MW00563613

A
RIGHT
VIEW *of*
YOURSELF

A RIGHT VIEW *of* YOURSELF

Rev. Fr. Frederick William Faber

TAN Books

Gastonia, North Carolina

MMXIX

This work has been derived, edited and arranged from *Growth in Holiness* by Rev. Fr. Frederick William Faber, first published in 1855.

Cover & interior design by www.davidferrisdesign.com

ISBN: 978-1-5051-1863-6
Kindle ISBN: 978-1-5051-1864-3
ePUB ISBN: 978-1-5051-1865-0

Published in the United States by

TAN Books
PO Box 269
Gastonia, NC 28053
www.TANBooks.com

Printed in the United States of America

CONTENTS

INTRODUCTION

TRAGIC SELF-KNOWLEDGE

The spiritual life is made up of contradictions. This is only another way of saying that human nature is fallen. One of the greatest contradictions, and practically one of the most difficult to be managed, is that in spirituality it is very important we should know a great deal about ourselves, and at the same time equally important that we should think very little about ourselves. No knowledge in the world can be more interesting to us than to know how we stand with God. Everything depends upon it. It is the true knowledge—indeed more than knowledge! If we are well with God, all is well with us, no matter how much trouble surrounds us. If we are not well with Him, nothing is well with us, no matter how wonderful things seem to be around us. This is a knowledge greater than the knowledge of good and evil which so violently tempted Adam and Eve. It is also natural—we should *want* to know if we are making progress in the spiritual life. When someone is in love, they desire to know that this love is accepted and reciprocated, and in the case of God, that it is not rejected as it deserves to be.

Why is this? Could it be that the divine beauty is so in love with us miserable creatures? Yet how shall we search the unsearchable loveliness of God? One momentary flash of His beauty would separate body and soul by the force of the ecstasy which it would cause, unless we were first fortified with the mysterious strength of the light of glory. Then, when we first wake in eternal glory, we shall see God before us in all His beauty, and in the light of His own incomprehensibility. He will be in the shapeliness of its own immensity, infinite light and infinite power, infinite wisdom with infinite sweetness, infinite joy and infinite glory, infinite majesty with infinite holiness, infinite riches with an infinite sea of being.

In the unity of a most transcending and majestic simplicity, and with limitless vision, we shall see the Divine Nature in its totality. Moreover, what we see, though we call it "it", is not a thing, but Him, a Being, Him, our Creator, Three Persons, One God. This Beauty is God, the beautiful God! O how we ourselves turn to dust and ashes, even to loathsome death and corruption, when we think of it!

Infinite wisdom must have strangely forgotten itself, if it can be in love with us for our own sakes. The most fearful thing about the divine wisdom, and that which makes it so adorable, is that it is God's knowledge of us in Himself. He does not look out upon us, and contemplate us, like an infinitely intelligent spectator on the outside. Rather, He looks into Himself, and sees us there, and knows us, as He knows all things in the highest, deepest, and most ultimate causes. He judges us with truth, which is an infallible light. But what is the self-knowledge of an examination of conscience, by the side of God's instantaneous, penetrating, and exhausting knowledge of us in Himself? That wisdom is also an endless abyss in which all the manifold beauties of possible creatures, and the magnificent worship of possible worlds, revolve in order, light, and number amidst the divine ideas. And what are we by the side of visions such as these? As the flood of the noon sun poured cruelly upon wounded eyes, so is the regard of God's knowledge fixed sternly on the sinner's soul. It must be an excruciating agony, added to the torments of the lost, to feel how nakedly and transparently they lie in the light of God's wisdom, before which no man can stand. Surely, we too have some faint shadow of that feeling? If the Sacred Humanity of Jesus did not cover our cold and nakedness and shivering poverty, as with a sacred mantle, or if we fell out from beneath it into the broad day of God's unsparing wisdom, we should surely faint away with fear and terror in the sense of our abject created vileness. Can we really dream that God loves us so much, because He knows us so thoroughly? O no! like little children must we hide our faces in the lap of our dearest Lord, and cry with half-stifled voice, "Turn away your face from my sins, and blot out all my iniquities!" Infinite wisdom has almost taxed itself with ingenious desires to save our souls and to win our love. What, in spite of all its curious array of graces find inventions, have we become? And how can that wisdom look upon us and be otherwise than disappointed? And what must disappointment be like, in God?

On our side, we are afflicted with a sense that everything is not right with us. In the first place, we are restless. We struggle with the movements of the spiritual life, and navigating prayer, mortification, idleness, and prayer. Then we experience an inability to resist temptations. We find ourselves going through the motions, as it were, with our penances and our devotional observances. Then we feel powerless to react to surprises which come upon us. We despair of sudden changes, in trials of temper, in the management of exterior duties, and the reconciliation of them with devotion and the interior life. Moreover, we are aware of a fundamental deficiency of inward light. Our examinations of conscience become foggy and misdirected. Temptations, being poorly met, cause in us an inclination to scruples, and so a littleness grows upon us. We seem to lose the sight of God which we had before, and which, imperfect as it was, was a true illumination. There is a vagueness about our spiritual combat which we feel requires a greater firmness, as well as more vigor. And added to all this, a sort of drowsy laziness is creeping over us like the oppression of a dream.

Something is wrong, it is clear; the question is, what? Here are three of these defects—ability, our reaction to temptations, and that inward light which must be accounted for. They arise from various causes. Partly they are the result of the attention we have been nearly forced to pay to ourselves and the interior experiences of our souls in these early stages of the spiritual life. Self-inspection is always dangerous, even when it is necessary.

Consequently, self-inspection should never be practiced without its proper accompanying antidote. Although self-knowledge is both a grace and a necessity and a blessing, none of these things prevent its also being a danger. The danger is in its leading us to unreality, sensitiveness, emotionalism, and that which is the most disgusting of vices in the spiritual life, sentimentality. It may be also that we have not exercised faith sufficiently, and this may account for the three defects in question. We have gone by feeling, or by sweetness, or by impulse, rather than by faith. In this way, we have mistaken God's gifts for God, and have accustomed our eyes to so strong an artificial light that we cannot see in the soft twilight which belongs to the Christian life. Or we have not been sufficiently careful in keeping ourselves in harmony with the spirit of the Church, neglecting certain devotions, or lightly esteeming them, such as confraternities, scapulars, indulgences and the like. Or we have not looked sufficiently out of ourselves to the objects of faith, but have rested on self-improvement too exclusively and too anxiously. Devotion can never neglect doctrine without paying dearly for it in the end. There is nothing Satan can clog our wheels with more effectually than an untheological devotion. Or again, our mistake may have arisen from our neglecting external works of mercy and edification, and our not being as careful as we should be in our dealings with others.

Thus, we shall now examine common paths and trials in acquiring self-knowledge—those things which must be managed well and those that must be wholly avoided, so as to come to a right view of our faults. In this way we will see where we stand before God.

—The Author

CHAPTER I

WHAT HOLDS US BACK

It seems now as if we had got our course clearly laid down, and had received our instructions as to the spirit in which we should serve God. We are fairly out of harbor, but how is it that we are not making way? We see others around us in full course, but no breeze is filling our sails. Whether it is that we are still under the influence of the shore, or whether it be that something else is in fault, it is clear that we are not catching the wind. Such is the common complaint of many souls at this period. Something holds them back; and they do not all at once see what it is. Our business now is to discover these secret obstacles, and see how to deal with them.

Our first step must be to examine the symptoms which betray that all is not right with us. As we have already said, something is wrong, but what? Were we not

1

ready for temptations? Was our devotion weak or insincere? What has made everything go cold?

Our secret obstacles consist of mistakes in our interior life as well as our exterior life. These mistakes are not sins, but places where we have not quite gone right on our journey without being properly aware of it. There are three common pitfalls in the interior life which we must look to before considering the outward problems.

1) It could be that what is holding us back is weak or improperly developed devotion to our Blessed Lady. Without this devotion an interior life is impossible. An interior life is one wholly conformed to the will of God; and our Blessed Lady is especially His will. She is the solidity of devotion. Yet this is not always sufficiently kept in mind. Beginners are often so busy with the mechanics of the spiritual life that they do not attribute sufficient importance to this devotion. Devotion to the Mother of Our Lord is not an ornament of the Catholic system, a prettiness, a superfluity, or even a help, out of many, which we may or may not use. It is an integral part of Christianity, and a religion is not, strictly speaking, Christian without it. It would be a different religion from the one God has revealed. Our Lady is a distinct ordinance of God, and a special means of grace, the importance of which is best tested by the intelligent wrath of the evil one against it and the instinctive hatred which heresy bears to it. She is the neck of the Mystical Body, uniting all the members with their Head. In this way, she is the channel and dispensing instrument of all graces. The devotion to her is the true

imitation of Jesus; for, next to the glory of His Father, it was the devotion nearest and dearest to His Sacred Heart. It is a peculiarly solid devotion, because it is perpetually occupied with the hatred of sin and the acquisition of substantial virtues. To neglect it is to despise God, for she is His ordinance, and to wound Jesus, because she is His Mother. God Himself has placed her in the Church as a distinct power, and hence she is operative, and a fountain of miracles, and a part of our religion which we can in no way ignore.

Spirituality must be orthodox. This is self-evident. Now doctrine which passes over the office and prerogatives of the Mother of God could not be orthodox. Thus, neither can spirituality be orthodox, if it be distinct or separable from a just devotion to her, and a devotion generous as well as just. Indeed, a mistake in doctrine is doubly dangerous when it is worked up into the spiritual life. It poisons everything, and there is no mischief which may not be predicted of the unfortunate soul which is the subject of it.

If then you have the symptoms of something wrong, something slowing you down, look first of all if your devotion to our Blessed Lady is all it ought to be. Is it deep enough? Is it true and fervent, or rather a necessary task that occupies as much attention in the heart as a household chore? Do you trust in the great power Christ has conferred upon His Blessed Mother? Are you truly devoted to her as one of her children? Perfection is under her peculiar patronage, because it is one of her special prerogatives as Queen of the Saints.

2) It may be that you need more devotion to the Sacred Humanity of Jesus and His mysteries. Even this is possible, and not so uncommon as we want to believe. Yet who could doubt that the devotion which may not leave us on the highest heights of contemplation, is quite indispensable in the states of the spiritual life which we are considering? It must permeate every part of the Christian life; and being a Christian means this, if it means anything. Christ is the Christian's way, the Christian's truth and the Christian's life. To lead a holy life is to be the Spouse of the Incarnate Word. Consequently, the love of the Incarnate Word is the very heart of holiness. The love of Christ's Sacred Humanity is manifested in three ways: *a)* one represents our interior affections toward Our Lord; *b)* another, the proofs of the sincerity and firmness of those affections; *c)* another the operations which Jesus Himself causes in the souls that are sufficiently well disposed. They are called, respectively: *affective, effective,* and *passive love.*

Affective love of our dear Lord consists in an intense desire for His glory, in a joyous complacency in the success of His interests, and in an affectionate, beautiful sorrow at the view of sin. It leads us to pour out our whole souls in confidence before Him, to complain of our coldness and imperfections, to put before Him our pains, weariness, disgust and trials, and to abandon all to Him with a quiet, childlike indifference.

Effective love makes us the living images of Jesus, representing in our own lives His states, His mysteries and, His virtues. We bear His image outwardly by continual mortification, by diminishing and narrowing our bodily comforts, by regulating our senses. Moreover, we bear it by cutting down the extravagant demands upon the world and society, and by a jealous moderation of innocent affections and pleasures. Lastly, by a perpetual repression of all vanity and conceit, which often inadvertently disguise with an apparent humility. Our interior life is conformed to Jesus by liberty of spirit, which means detachment from creatures and conformity to His will. Our external actions have His character stamped upon them when we act as His members, and all our actions are done in dependence upon Him, and according to His movement.

Passive love. In this consideration, I mean for us to learn to thirst for what one day may be ours, more than what, ordinarily speaking, something to look for at this early stage of the spiritual life. It is a happy thing to see how close, please God, we may one day be to Jesus even before we die. His first operation in this supernatural state is to wound our souls with love, so that we lose our taste for everything which is not Him or His. It is as if a new nature were given us, so little in harmony with the wretched world around us, that we languish and pine, as out of our proper element. Then, He deepens the wound, and causes all our thoughts, affections, words and works to be imbued with His love, until we are unable to do anything but seek after Him, like the Spouse in the *Canticles.* Every love is renounced but His, every idea effaced from our minds but of Him, and everything unrelated to Him disappears from our memory as though it had never been.

In this way, He possesses our soul altogether, and it is not so much we who live as He who lives in us. Then He sets us all on fire with resistless love, and makes us break out into actions of heroic charity and supernatural union with Him, while all the time He so deepens in us the sense of our own vileness and nothingness that we do nothing but deplore the meanness of our service and the dullness of our hearts. Lastly, He throws us into a state of purifying suffering, and fastens on our shoulders the perpetual Cross, when we seek for nothing but to suffer more, and shrink from nothing but to suffer less. So, He strips us of ourselves, and makes us wholly His. But all this is a long way on. Look up and strain your eyes. I do not know that you will so much as see the mountaintops where all this will be found. But don't despair! It is something to know that those fair heights are really there.

We cannot imagine what advantages we derive from these exercises of love of the Incarnate Word. The heart detaches itself from creatures; self-love burns down and goes out; imperfections are corrected; the soul is filled with the spirit of Jesus, and advances with giant strides along the paths of perfection. See then, if you are getting nowhere, whether your love of Our Lord's adorable Person and Sacred Humanity is all it should be, all He meant and all He asks, or at least whether you are distinctly cultivating it, and doing your best daily to make it grow.

3) The third deficiency, which is probably by far the most common, may be a lack of childlike feeling toward God. I wish I could be very clear, as well as very strong,

about this, because so very much depends upon it. If our view of God is not uniformly and habitually that of a Father, the very fountains of piety will be corrupted within us. We shall incur the woe of which the Prophet speaks; our sweet will be bitter, and our bitter sweet.

Our position toward God is that of creatures. Let us see more how this works. We belong absolutely to Him. We have no rights but those which He compassionately chooses to secure to us by covenant. Our life is at the mercy of providence, and providence is not a mere course of external events, but the significant will of Three Divine Persons, One God. Our condition in the next life is known to Him already; and we on our part know that more grace than He is obliged to give is necessary for us, although we know of an infallible certainty that He will give it us, if we choose to correspond to what we have. Yet this last consideration cannot wholly allay the nervousness which the view of our position naturally causes us. Reflection on the attributes of God, His omniscience, omnipotence, immensity and ineffable holiness, is not calculated to diminish this feeling. Nevertheless the conviction that the spirit of adoration, the temper of worship, the instinct of religiousness, reside simply in our always feeling, speaking, and acting toward God as creatures, that is, as beings who have no independent existence but have been called out of nothing by Him, is in reality so far from projecting a gloomy shadow over us, or exciting an internal disquietude, that the more seriously these truths are received into the soul, and the more unreservedly we acknowledge the sovereignty of God, the more calming, supernaturally calming, will their effect be found.

Yet this does not appear on the surface, nor will it, until the mind has become accustomed to religious thought, and I daresay imbued with it. We are tempted to look at God in almost any light rather than that of a Father, as well because of our own helplessness as His overpowering immensity and omnipotence. Yet our spiritual life depends entirely on the view we take of God. If we look at Him as our Master, then His service is our task, and the ideas of reward and punishment will pervade all we do. If we regard Him as our King, surely, we must be crushed by the indubitable rights of His unquestionable rule, and nothing more tender than an abstraction of dutiful loyalty may we dare to cherish in our hearts. If we look at Him as our Judge, the thunders of His vengeance deafen us, the awful exactness of His indictment strikes us dumb, while the splendor of His intolerable sanctity blinds us. If we consider Him exclusively, in any one of these lights, or in all of them, it is plain our service to Him will take its character from our views. Hardness, dryness, pure fear and a consciousness of our being unable to stand upon our rights will necessarily make us cowardly and mean, cringing and mercenary, querulous and as disrespectful as we dare to be.

But we may even look at Him as our Creator, and yet be wrong. For it is possible to consider a Creator to be an independent and eternally self-existing Being, who for His own good pleasure, as First Cause, has called creatures out of nothing, and cares as little for them as He is beholden to them.

Yet it should be plain that to be a Creator implies being a Father too. The very will of Creation is surely a stupendous act of paternal tenderness. Thus, God is not only our Father and our Creator also, but He is our Father because He is our Creator. A rational creature, to be a creature, must be a son also. We bring with us out of our primal nothingness the filial bond. Creation ranges itself rather under goodness than under power or wisdom. So that if I knew no more of God than that He was my Creator, I ought to feel that He was my Father also. *Qui plasmasti me miserere mei*—You who formed me, have mercy on me, was the lifelong prayer of the penitent of the desert. There was a sort of right, or a sound of right, in the very appellation, which endeared it to her lowliness and timidity.

At any rate, there is no truth more certain than that God is our Father. All that is most tender and most gentle in all paternity on earth is but the merest shadow of the boundless sweetness and affectionateness of His paternity in Heaven. The beauty and consolation of this idea surpass words. It destroys the sense of loneliness in the world and puts a new color on chastisement and affliction. It calls consolation out of the very sense of weakness, and enables us to trust God for the problems we cannot solve, while binding us by a sense of most dear relationship to all our fellowmen. The idea enters into and becomes the master thought of even all our spiritual actions. In sin, we remember it, while on the other hand, moving toward perfection we lean upon it. In temptations we feed upon it, and in suffering we enjoy it. He is our Father in the ordinary events of life, which entails protection from a thousand evils which He never lets us feel, as well as in answers to prayer, and in blessing those we love. We feel it in forbearance with ourselves, forbearance with a degree of coldness and incorrigibleness which is almost incredible, even to ourselves.

He is our Father not in name only, but truly. As I said, the bond comes out of creation. The Creator has a marvelous and mysterious sensible love for His creatures, with which no earthly affection can compare for indulgence or for tenderness. He has been pleased to make our interests identical with His, and He has so created us in His likeness and image as that we should reflect even His Divine Majesty. But He is our Father also by covenant; and as He ever effects what He promises, this new paternity is as real as the other. And beyond all ties of nature, grace and glory, by which He calls us children, He is our Father in a way we can never fully know, in that He is the Father of Our Lord Jesus Christ.

Out of this filial feeling toward our heavenly Father comes ease of conscience as to past sin. We can trust Him, in sweet confidence, even with the unutterable decision of our eternal doom. We enjoy liberty of spirit in indifferent actions, mingled with an intense desire to serve Him which our filial love inspires. Out of it come also a sweet forgetfulness of self, enjoyment in prayer, patience in doubts, calmness in difficulties, lightheartedness in trials and an uncomplaining contentment in desolation. We worship Him for His own blessed sake, because He is our dear Father. Happy sunshine of this thought! It falls upon our souls with triple beam, more trust in God, more freedom with God, more generosity with God!

Above all, we should be thoroughly imbued with the true spirit of the Gospel. That men so frequently miss it, is partly owing to their not remembering every hour of the day that our Blessed Lord is God, and partly to their mixing some other idea of God with that of Father, and allowing the harsher element to dominate. The spirit of the Gospel is tenderness. Now, these three deficiencies, of devotion to Our Lady, of devotion to the Sacred Humanity and of childlike trust in God, are at once effects of a lack of tenderness, and causes of the continued defect. This is the great hidden hindrance. With your bold desire for perfection, your disgust with the world and your appreciation of high things, you expect to be making progress, and are disappointed. I have already asked you to look at yourselves and see whether you are not lacking in devotion to our Blessed Lady, to our dear Lord's Sacred Humanity and to the ever-blessed Paternity of God. Now let me put it in another shape. A deficiency of these three things means in reality a lack of tenderness, though it means other things as well. But the absence of tenderness in religion is often of itself enough to stay man's growth in holiness. It is worthwhile, therefore, to say something on this head. A man may be in a certain sense religious. He may fear God, hate sin, be strictly conscientious and honestly desire to save his soul. All these are most excellent things. But you cannot say that the Saints were men of this sort. Nor were they plaster saints whose faces would crack were they to smile. They had about them a sweetness, a softness, a delicacy, a gentleness, an affectionateness, and truly, a poetry, which gave quite a different character to their devotion. They were living images of Jesus. This, in our far inferior measure and degree, we also must strive to be, if we would grow in holiness.

Tenderness does not mean a mere impressionableness, softheartedness or a facility of tears. These are as often marks of cowardice, laziness and a want of resolute will and earnestness. True tenderness begins in various ways. Its progress is marked by a sorrow for sin, without thinking of its punishment, by what I have elsewhere called a touchiness about the interests of Jesus, by childlike docility to our superiors and spiritual directors, by mortifying ourselves and not feeling it a burden. It is marked by never thinking of stopping short at precepts without going on to counsels, and by a very faint, incipient, and as yet scarcely discernible appetite for humiliations. In proportion to how it is formed in our souls, all the characteristics of sanctity gather to it and group themselves round it. For love is a greater safeguard against sin than fear, and tenderness renders our conversion with God more whole by making it easier. It especially attracts Jesus, whose Spirit it is, and who will not be outdone in His own peculiar sweetness. Without this tenderness there can be no growth. Then, while it renders duty more easy, and consequently the performance of duty more perfect, it instills into us the especially Christian like instincts such as love of suffering, silence under injustice, a thirst for humiliations and the like. Moreover, it deepens sorrow for sin into a contrition which is worth more to the penitent soul than any gift that can be named. Look at the phenomena of the Incarnation—what are they? Helplessness, unnecessary and unobliged suffering, sacrifice, abasement, continual defeat, no assertion of rights, carelessness of success and most pathetic wrongs. And what is our response to all these things, but the temper which is expressed by that one word, tenderness?

The Sacred Infancy, the Passion, the Blessed Sacrament, and the Sacred Heart teaches tenderness. But look at the common life of Jesus among men, and you will see more clearly what this tenderness is like. There is first the tenderness of Our Lord's outward deportment. The narrative of Palm Sunday is an instance of it. Also, His way with His disciples, His way with sinners and His way with those in affliction or grief who threw themselves in His road. He did not quench the smoking flax, nor break the bruised reed. This was a complete picture of Him. There was tenderness in His very looks, as when He looked on the rich young man and loved him, or when St. Peter was converted by a look. His whole conversation was imbued with tenderness. The tone of His parables, the absence of terrors in His sermons, and the abyss of forgiveness which His teaching opens out, all exemplify this. He is no less tender in His answer to questions, as when He was accused of being possessed, and when He was struck on the face. His very reprimands were steeped in tenderness; witness the woman taken in adultery, James and John, and the Samaritan, and Judas. Nor was His zeal less tender, as was evidenced when He rebuked the brothers who would fain have called down fire from Heaven upon the Samaritan villagers, and also by the sweet meekness of His divine indignation when He cleared the Temple.

Now if Our Lord is our model, and if His Spirit be ours, it is plain that a Christian-like tenderness must make a deep impression upon our spiritual life, and indeed give it its principal tone and character. Without tenderness we can never have that spirit of generosity in which we saw that we must serve God. It is as necessary to our interior life, or our relation with God, as it is to our exterior life or relation with others. There is one gift of the Holy Spirit, namely piety, whose special office it is to confer this tenderness.

If then the secret obstacles of which you complain concern your interior life, and arise from defects in your devotional feelings and exercises, cultivate these three devotions: to our Blessed Lady, to the Sacred Humanity of Jesus and to the Paternity of God, and great results will follow. Put yourself right in these three things, and the sails will no longer idly flap against the mast.

CHAPTER 2

OUR NORMAL STATE

Everything in the world seems to have a peculiar beginning and a peculiar ending, with a normal state between them. It is always this normal state which gives the truest character of a thing, for it expresses its nature and ruling idea. Yet the phenomena of the spiritual life appear to be of a different kind. It seems at first sight as if the spiritual life could have no normal state, except being a perpetual dissatisfied progress, whose highest mark would always be a disappointment, as falling so far below even reasonable and legitimate expectation.

The greater part of its time and attention is taken up with mere preliminaries. What with means, vigilance, reparations, commandments, prohibitions and warnings, almost the whole of a spiritual book is occupied with studying the chart, rather than starting us on our voyage.

The last chapter of many books gets no further than a fall launch. Then it seems as if we never did get into a fixed state, such as we could call normal or habitual. What follows no rule can give no rule; how then can it be normal? Fallen nature cannot go to God either in a groove or down an inclined plane, any more than men can march through a hilly country or fight a battle on mathematical lines.

Moreover, the experiences of the Saints are nothing more than a continually shifting scene of vicissitudes, and alternations of bright and dark, which baffle all induction, so various, perplexing, unruly and contradicting are they. Even as a panorama gradually unfolded, the spiritual life has no apparent unity, completeness or dramatic completion. As a journey it is up-hill. Its paths, therefore, like all mountain tracks, devious, winding and seemingly capricious. Hence there is no feeling of working up to a table-land, where we may hope to try other sinews and enjoy the level.

Yet for all this the spiritual life has a kind of normal state; and we shall find the knowledge of it a help to us. It consists in a perpetual interchange of three dispositions, sometimes succeeding each other and reigning in turns, sometimes two of them occupying the throne at once, and sometimes all three at the same time exercising their influence conjoined. These three dispositions are struggle, fatigue and rest. Each of them requires an attendant satellite to give them light in the night-time of their revolutions. Struggle requires patience. Fatigue must be proof against human respect. Rest must lean upon mortification, for nowhere else can she safely sleep. Now we will look a little more closely at the dispositions which make up our normal state.

I must speak first of struggle. There seems theoretically to be no difficulty in this idea, yet practically it is not an easy one to realize. If the tradition of the Universal Church is harmonious and conclusive on any one point concerning the spiritual life, it is that it is a struggle, strife, combat, battle, warfare, whichever word you may choose. No one doubts it. A man would be out of his senses if he were to doubt it. Reason proves it, authority proves it, experience proves it. Yet see what an awkward practical question for each one of us rises out of this universal admission. At any moment we may turn round upon ourselves and say, "Is my religious life a struggle? Do I feel it to be so? What am I struggling against? Do I see my enemy? Do I feel the weight of his opposition? If my life is not sensibly a fight, can it be a spiritual life at all? Or rather am I not in one of the common delusions of easy devotion and unmortified effeminacy?" If I am not fighting, I am conquered; and surely, I can hardly be fighting, and not know it. These are very serious questions to ask ourselves, and we ought to be frightened if at any time we cannot obtain satisfactory answers to them. A good frightening! What an excellent thing it is now and then in the spiritual life! Yet in these times it seems as if we were all to be invalids in holiness. Spiritual direction expends its efforts in producing a composing silence round about our sickbeds, as if the great thing was not to awake us; and the little table near has a tiny opiate for each devout scruple as it rises, to lay it to sleep again, as if it were not true that these scruples are often, like the irritability of a patient, signs of returning strength. Is simple convalescence from mortal sin to be the model holiness of our day, at least for luckless souls living in the world?

Oh, how one comes to love a great huge city like London, when God has thrown us into it as our vineyard! The monster! It looks so unmanageable, and it is positively so awfully wicked, so hopelessly magnificent, so heretically wise and proud after its own fashion. Yet after a fashion it is good also. Such a multitudinous remnant who have never bowed the knee to Baal, such numbers seeking their way to the light, such hearts touched by grace, so much secret holiness, such supernatural lives, such loyalty, mercy, sacrifice, sweetness, greatness! St. Vincent Ferrer preached in its streets, and Father Colombiere in its suburbs. Do not keep down what is good in it, only because it is trying to be higher. Help people to be saints. Not all who ask for help really wish it, when it comes to be painful. But some do. Raise ten souls to detachment from creatures, and to close union with God, and what will happen to this monster city? Who can tell? Monster as it is, it is not altogether unamiable. It means well often, even when it is cruel. Well-meaning persons are unavoidably cruel. Yet it is often as helpless and as deserving of compassion as it is of wrath and malediction. Poor Babylon! would she might have a blessing from her unknown God, and that grace might find its way even into her Areopagus!

18

But what does our struggle consist of? Mostly of five things; and if there were time for it, we might write a chapter on each of them. First, there is positive fighting. You see I am letting you off easily, for some would say that the Christian life is always a fight, even an actual battle; and that doctrine, sought to be verified in your practice, might often be very discouraging. I call it a struggle, and I make positive fighting only one part of it. Secondly, there is taking pains, such as pitching tents, cleaning arms, gathering fuel, cooking rations, reconnoitering. Thirdly, there are forced marches. If I ask you whether you are fighting, and you answer, No, but I am footsore, I shall be quite content, and will not tease you anymore. I do not even object to an occasional bivouac; it all comes into my large and generous sense of the word warfare.

Fourthly, there is a definite enemy. By this I do not mean that you must always know your enemy when you see him. A vice may come and play the spy in the clothes of a dead virtue. But you must have an enemy in view, and know what you are about with him. To invade the world, and then look round for an enemy, is not the businesslike thing I understand by the spiritual combat. Fifthly, there must be an almost continual sensible strain upon you, whichever of your military duties you may be performing. If you feel no differently on your battlefield from what you used to feel in the hay field, you will not come up to my mark. These are the five things of which our struggle consists.

But you will ask, what are the enemies against whom I have to struggle? Seven; and the natural history of each of them might occupy a little treatise by itself. We must now dispatch them with a few words. First, we have to fight against sin, not only with actual temptations in times when they press us hard, but at all times with the habits which old sins have wound so tightly and so fearfully around us, and with the weakness which is a consequence of our past defeats. The reason why men are so often surprised into grave sins is not always to be found in the vehemence of the temptation, and their want of attention to it at the time, but in their want of attention to the general moral weakness which past and even forgiven sin has left behind it.

Secondly, we must struggle with temptations, and we must struggle with them with amazing courage, not as foes whose lines we have to break, and then the country will be clear before us, but as foes who will thicken as we advance. The weakest come first, at least if we except those which tried to hinder our giving ourselves up to God at the first. The stronger come next. The robustness of our temptations seems to be in proportion to our growth in grace. The choicest are kept to the last. We shall one day have to give battle to the pretorians, to the devil's bodyguard; and probably it will be when we are lying, white and weak, on a deathbed. We must bear this in mind about temptations, else we shall make too much of our victories, and be disheartened by the smallness of their results. No victory that we gain is worth anything to the victories we have yet to gain. Still, a victory is always a victory.

Our third enemies are our trials. Our trials, like our temptations, grow as we advance. We are forcing our way into a more difficult country. We see evil where we did not see it before. In this way, we have more things to avoid than formerly. We are attempting greater things, and climbing higher hills. All this has its encouraging side. But then in proportion to the greatness and the height, so is the difficulty. Then holiness has a whole brood of trials and troubles of its own, the like to which do not exist in the free-living, easy-mannered, fair-spoken world. Its interior trials are enough of themselves to keep a stout saint occupied all his life long. What is necessary to remember is that we have not faced our worst yet. We must not cry victory when the battle is in truth but just begun.

Fourthly, we have to struggle against the changes of our own faults. After all, there is something very comfortable in a habit, when once the labor of acquiring it has been surmounted. We have got into a particular way, and it is a trouble to be put out of it. Improvements in tools only make them more awkward at first to old workmen. David felt so little at ease in Saul's armor, that he went back to his shepherd's dress and his favorite old sling. It is the same with us. We get into a certain way with ourselves, a certain hatred of ourselves, and a certain severity with ourselves. It was hard to get used to it; but we did so at last, and now do pretty well. Then by age or outward circumstances, or through some interior crisis, our faults change, and we have a new warfare to learn. Moreover, these changes of our faults are often imperceptible at the time. We are not conscious of what is going on. And as our characters sometimes turn right around, we may go on neglecting something which we ought to observe, and observing something we may now safely neglect; nay, we may even be playing the game of some new passion, while we think we are mortifying old ones. This is a perplexity. It annoys and distracts us in our struggle, even if it does nothing more. We must be prepared for it.

Teasing imperfections are our fifth enemy. The warfare against them is neither dangerous nor dignified—but wearing, harassing and annoying. Certain infirmities seem at times to be endowed with a supernatural vitality, and will not be put down even by our most earnest and persevering efforts. Habits of carelessness in saying the Divine Office or the Rosary, slight immortifications at meals, the use of particular expressions, matters connected with external composure and recollection, are all instances of this at times. It seems annoying that we should be in bondage to such very little things, and it is a trial both of faith and temper. But God sometimes allows that we should entirely miss our aim when striking at them, in order that our devotion may be hidden from the eyes of others, who might wither it by praise, or that we ourselves should bear about a thorn in the flesh, as the Apostle did, to keep us humble and make us truly despise ourselves. Perhaps grace is often saved under the shadow of an imperfection. There are many imperfections which are more obvious and humiliating than really guilty or unworthy in the sight of God. Under any circumstances, the tiresome struggle with our imperfections will not end, even with Extreme Unction. It will cease only with our breath, only when we are actually laid to rest in the bosom of our indulgent and heavenly Father.

The sixth object with which we have to struggle is the subtraction of divine light and sensible aid, whether it come upon us as a purifying trial or as a chastisement for unfaithfulness. This is like Jacob's struggle when he wrestled with God; or rather it is a wrestling with God, self, and the evil one, all at once. For no sooner does God withdraw His sensible assistance from us than the devil attacks us with renewed violence, and we ourselves give way to wounded self-love and to despondency. It is with us as with the Israelites in Egypt: we have more bricks to make, and the straw is not to be found as it used to be. At least it seems so. Yet God is with us when we know it not. We could not so much as hold on, if He were not. But it is hard to realize this with a sheer and simple faith, when sensation and sentiment are quite the other way. Mercifully this struggle is not perpetual. It comes and goes, and if we could get ourselves to look on it beforehand as a significant visitation of mysterious love, we should be able to bear up against it more gently and more manfully than we do. Ordinarily we weary ourselves too much of violent effort, and then lie helpless and supine in a kind of petulant despair. Losing our temper with God is a more common thing in the spiritual life than many men suppose. It dashes back to earth many a rising prayer, and vitiates many a brave mortification. Happy they who can wrestle with God in uncomplaining prayer, in self-collected reverence, and yet by His grace with the vigorous will to have the better of Him. This brings me to the seventh enemy with whom we have to struggle. It is familiarity; and familiarity especially with three things: prayer, Sacraments and temptations. As I have said before, to have relations with God is a very fearful thing.

To love God is a bold and arduous thing. It was of His compassion that He made that to be of precept which was in itself so unspeakable a privilege. Yet it is hard to love warmly and tenderly, and to love reverently as well. Hence it is that, with so many, familiarity fastens upon love, and blights it. Familiarity in prayer consists of meditating without preparing, of using words without weighing them, of slouching postures, of indeliberate epithets, of peevish complaint, and of lightly making the petitions of saints our own. All this is an intolerable familiarity with the great majesty of God. It grows upon us. Use brings slovenliness, and slovenliness makes us profane. Familiarity with the Sacraments consists in going to Confession with a very cursory examination, and a mere flying act of contrition, making no thanksgiving afterwards and setting no store by our penance; as if we were privileged people, and were entitled to take liberties with the Precious Blood.

With the Blessed Eucharist it consists of frequent Communion without leave, or forcing leave, or making no preparation, or careless thanksgiving, as if forsooth our whole life were to be considered adequate preparation and adequate thanksgiving, and that it shows liberty of spirit to be on such free and easy terms with the Adorable Sacrament. Familiarity with temptations is to lose our horror of their defiling character, to be remiss and dilatory in repelling them, to feel our loathing of them diminish, not to be sufficiently afraid of them, and to take for granted that we are so established in any particular virtue that our falling is out of all question. These familiarities grow upon us like the insidious approaches of sleep. We feel an increasing reluctance to throw them off and shake them from us. It will not be so much the thoughts of Hell and Purgatory, wholesome as they are, which will keep us right, as frequent meditation on the adorable attributes of God. If our flesh were but always pierced with the arrows of holy fear, how much more angelic would our lives become!

CHAPTER 3

FATIGUE

The next disposition in which our normal state resides is fatigue. This is something more than the pleasant feeling of being tired. Indeed, if there is pleasure in it sometime, it is far more often a weary and oppressive pain. For the fatigue of which I speak is caused by the struggle which we have just been considering. It consists first of faintness, which the mere continuity of the combat superinduces. Secondly, of disgust, a loathing for all sacred things; thirdly, of irritability, not only from frequent defeat, but from the harassing nature of the warfare; fourthly, of low spirits, especially when the arm of grace is less sensibly upholding us; and fifthly, of a feeling of the impossibility of persevering, which is not despair, because we do not cease our efforts, only we make them with the mere force of the grace-assisted will, not with the hope and energy of the heart. This fatigue may obviously be felt during a battle as well as after it: and as we may both offend God, and also do very foolish things injurious to our own interests, under the heavy hand of this fatigue, it is important for us to get a clear idea of it, and to investigate its causes.

These causes are seven in number, and each of them is accompanied by its own peculiar trials, dangers and temptations. The first cause is the constant opposition to nature which the spiritual life implies. I am not speaking so much of voluntary mortification, though that also must be taken into the account. But everything we do in the spiritual life is contrary to the will and propensions of our corrupt nature. There is no pleasure to which we dare yield an unlimited assent. There is no spiritual enjoyment which is not more or less a suffering to our poor nature. What a joy is prayer; yet to nature mortification even is less irksome than prayer. Our tastes, wishes, inclinations, instincts, what we seek and what we shun, are all more or less thwarted by the effort to be holy. When nature offers us any assistance, we doubt her and suspect her intentions, and when we use the force she supplies, we do it in a harsh, ungraceful manner toward her. Her very activity, which is the making of so many of us, we regard almost as an enemy, hurrying us as it does out of the calm presence of God, and into endless indiscretions. The custody of the senses, even such an amount of it as is an absolute duty, is a bondage which nature is hardly able to bear. In a word, in proportion as grace takes possession of us, we grow out of sympathy with our own very nature, and in some respects with the outward creation generally. This becomes visible to the eye when it reaches the point which it does often attain in saints and ecstatic persons. Their illnesses, sufferings and apparently unnatural valetudinarian states are simply the result of the supernatural and mystical character of their lives. As mystical theologians teach, the nutritive, nervous and cerebral systems are all deranged by the entire possession which grace has taken of the soul, especially in those whose lives are contemplative and interior. But this begins in a slight measure, as soon as we commence the spiritual life in good earnest, and it must obviously produce fatigue. The mere rowing against the stream perpetually must make us stiff and tired. And not only can there be no peace with nature, but, except in an ecstasy, no truce either; and from what the Saints tell us, it appears that nature takes a terrific vengeance on them for their ecstasies, when they are passed.

A second cause of fatigue is in the uncertainty in which temptation so often leaves us, as to whether we have consented or not. To walk blindfolded or to find our way in the dark is in itself a tiring thing. Clear light mitigates fatigue. But when we are uncertain whether we have offended God or not, whether such or such an action was against our vows or resolutions, we lose our elasticity. If we have really conquered, we have no sense of victory to buoy us up; and if we were vanquished, we should be better able to face the disaster manfully, if there was no doubt about it. But as a mile's walk with the sun in our faces or the dust in our eyes is longer than ten without such annoyances, so is it with this uncertainty which temptation casts over us in spite, as it goes away. It tires and unnerves us.

A third cause of fatigue is to be found in the daily monotonous renewal of the combat. Sameness is wearisome in itself. This is in great measure the wretchedness of imprisonment, no matter how comfortable and roomy our dungeon may be. The sun shines through our window, the morning breeze comes there, and the little birds sing outside. For a moment our waking thoughts do not realize where we are or what we have to encounter. But when we are fully aware that we have another day before us of uncheckered monotonous confinement, the soul sinks within us, forlorn and weary, even after long hours of refreshing sleep. So it is in the spiritual life. Is it to be always combat? Will the pressure ever be taken off?

Is the strain never to be relaxed? Is the hold never to be let go? And when we are obliged to answer ourselves with the simple "Never," this hourly renewal of the old, old strife becomes almost insupportable. Take any one besetting infirmity, for instance want of government of the tongue, or unworthy pleasure in eating and drinking, how jaded and disgusted we become long before we have made any sensible impression upon the strength of the evil habit!

A fourth cause of fatigue is in the little progress we make in a long time. Success hinders fatigue. The excitement carries us on, and supplies fresh forces to nature, enabling her to draw on the secret funds of her constitution, which, otherwise, nothing but the death-struggle would have brought out.

On the contrary, defeat is akin to listlessness. Besides this, slow walking is more tiring than fast. Men hurry up and down a short quarterdeck, because a funeral pace makes them low-spirited and footsore. These are all types of what the spirit feels. Our small progress deprives us of all natural encouragement.

For our minds must be thoroughly saturated with supernatural principles, always to realize that one evil thought repelled, one angry humor smartly chastised, one base envy well warred down, one thorough *Deo gratias* in a piece of ill luck, may be really hundreds of leagues of progress. Each of them is worth more than the whole world to us, as something which pleases God, and which God alone has enabled us to do. Unfortunately, we usually realize our supernatural principles most when we feel fatigue least; and it is for this reason that our slow progress is so wearisome. A calm at sea is fatiguing, even though no physical effort is called for on our part. To scale Parnassus in the face of a blustering wind and a drenching rain is less tiring than to rock idly and helplessly for a day in the Gulf of Corinth, with beauty enough in sight to feed mind and eye for weeks.

The fifth cause of fatigue is the universality of vigilance which is required in the spiritual life. We have not only to be always on the alert, but our watchfulness has such a wide extent of ground to cover. Everything else in the spiritual life we can concentrate, except our vigilance; and that we cannot concentrate. The nearest approach to it is the practice of particular examen of conscience, quite one of the most helpful and operative practices of the spiritual life. But that is not in reality so much a concentration of our vigilance, as that the fixing our attention very earnestly on one fault helps to keep us awake, and makes our eyes quick to see anything stir and our ears sharp for the slightest sound. And who will say that particular examination is not fatiguing in itself? He is a happy man who keeps to it without missing, for as much as one single moon. Truly vigilance is a tiring thing in itself: what then must it be, when we add to it universality and uninterruptedness? Yet such is the vigilance the world, the flesh and the devil exact from us continually. Liberty of spirit is a mighty boon. It dispenses with many things. But woe be to him who dreams that it dispenses him from watchfulness!

A sixth cause of fatigue is in the mere wear and tear of duration. A light work will tire, if it is sufficiently prolonged, and the work of the spiritual life is simply unending—the pressure of it continuous. It is true that this fatigue is easier to bear than some of the others, because there is something consoling in the thought that we have persevered so far.

Nevertheless, it forms one of the difficulties of perseverance. For while we feel fatigued at the present moment, the future presents us with no other prospect. A lifelong vista of work stretches before us: long or short as it may please God; still always work. There is no retiring on a pension or half-pay from the military service of the spiritual life.

Seventh is fatigue that is generated by fatigue itself. We get tired of being tired. And this produces a sort of torpor most dangerous to the soul. We become indifferent to things. We grow callous to the feeling of our own unworthiness, to the horror of sin, to the glorious desirableness of God and of union with Him. We are like a broken musical instrument. We give no sound when we are fingered. There is something in this state analogous to the swept and garnished heart of which our Savior speaks, into which seven devils might easily enter, worse than the first who had been ejected from it. The only safety in this kind of fatigue is more occupation. We must burden still more the already overburdened spirit. This remedy requires faith. Nothing but snow itself will draw the frost out of the bitten limbs of the sealer of the Antarctic. It is a cruel cure, but a specific. So, it is with this tiring of being tired. If you do not load it more, even to making it restless, angry, rebellious, if you will, in a short time you will be on the brink of seriously throwing up the service of God altogether.

These are our seven fatigues; and I am almost afraid of what I have written. I fear lest it should discourage you. Alas! it is not the truest kindness to throw a false rose-colored light over the harsh and rocky portions of the spiritual landscape.

Man must not represent as wholly easy, what God has made in part most difficult. But you must remember, this is only one side of the picture, and the dark side. I have put it at the worst, for I have assumed throughout that God uniformly subtracted sensible sweetness and interior consolation from you all the while. Yet this is hardly ever so, perhaps never, and certainly never with any souls to whom He has not first given immense gifts of courage, fortitude and endurance, or a peculiar attraction to walk by faith only. Later, you will see how to avoid the dangers with which this fatigue is fraught. We must not fail to remember that the spiritual joys of holiness far more than counterbalance its fatigue, and secondly, that whatever you do, I counsel you not to rush from the momentary and apparent dullness and uninterestingness of the things of God to seek refuge and consolation in creatures. The consequences of such a step are dreadful. I had almost said irremediable. But I have seen things which show that it is not quite irremediable. I hope no mistake of any kind in the spiritual life is irremediable. The case of a tepid religious has been quoted as such. But we know that even such cases are curable, because they have been cured. And what can be incurable if they are not?

CHAPTER 4

IDLENESS

In considering our normal state, we need to look to a great difficulty, namely idleness. Although I say it is a difficulty, I suppose it may be said that every man is an idle man.

Did anyone ever see a man who did not naturally gravitate to idleness, unless perchance he had a heart complaint? Rather, it is so natural, that very idle men plead its very naturalness as a proof that it is almost irresistible. No man does hard work naturally. He must be driven to it, no matter whether it be by the love of money, or the fear of Hell. Idleness of its own nature is sweet, sweeter than the brightest gift the happy world can give. But spiritual men have a special inclination to be idle, which they do not always sufficiently consider.

Nothing is rarer in the Church than a true contemplative vocation. Consequently, it is almost impossible for the generality of devout persons to spend their whole time in direct acts of the virtue of religion, and the cultivation of interior motives and dispositions. Then, on the other hand, they conceive, not always judiciously, that their former habits of recreation, and their old amusements, are to be altogether eschewed.

So that their piety creates a sort of void in them, and gives them nothing to fill it up with. This is one great reason why those who have no regular profession, or adequate domestic occupation, should engage themselves in some external work of zeal and mercy. However, if this theory to explain the phenomenon be not true, the fact is undeniable, and the world has long ill-naturedly pointed to it, that religious people, as a class, are uncommonly idle. As this idleness is an effectual bar to progress, it is important that we should examine the matter narrowly; and if we do so, we shall find that there are many developments of this spiritual idleness, about each of which something shall be said.

The first of them is what is usually called dissipation. It is easy to describe, but not easy to define. It is a sin without a body. It can make a body of anything and animate it. It works quietly, and hardly allows itself to be felt. Indeed, one of its most dangerous characteristics is that a person is rarely aware, at the time, that he is guilty of dissipation. Its effects upon our devotion are quite disproportioned to the insignificance of its appearance. It can destroy in a few hours the hard-earned graces of months, or the fruit of a whole retreat; and the time immediately following a retreat is one of its favorite and chosen seasons. Let us see in what it consists. Everyone knows after he has been dissipated that such has been the case; but he does not always see in what his dissipation has consisted. The desolation of his soul is a proof to him that something has been wrong; but he cannot always give the wrong its name.

Dissipation consists, first of all, in putting things off beyond their proper times. So that one duty treads upon the heels of another, and all duties are felt as irksome obligations, a yoke beneath which we fret and lose our peace. In most cases the consequence of this is that we have no time to do the work as it ought to be done. It is therefore done precipitately, with natural eagerness, with a greater desire to get it simply done than to do it well, and with very little thought of God throughout.

The great thing is to do each duty as it comes, quietly, perseveringly and with our eyes fixed on God. Without our having any set rule to observe, daily life has a tendency to settle itself into a groove, and thus each duty has a time which may be called its right time; and by observing this we shall avoid, on the one hand, being pressed by an accumulation of duties in arrear, and on the other being dissipated by having gaps of time not filled up. An unoccupied man can neither be a happy man nor a spiritual man.

Another symptom of dissipation consists in over-talking and prolonging immoderately visits of civility. By this is not meant that there is any point at which a person is bound to stop, or where anything positively wrong begins; but that there is such a thing as moderation in those matters, which is guided in each case by circumstances. Again, indulging in idle and indolent postures of body when we are alone tends to dissipate the mind and weakens the hold which the presence of God ought to have upon us. We must also be upon our guard against a habit, which is far from uncommon, of being always about to begin some occupation, and yet not beginning it.

This wastes our moral strength, and causes us to fritter our lives away in sections, being idle today because we have something in view tomorrow, which cannot be begun until tomorrow. The same dissipating result will be produced if we burden ourselves with too many vocal prayers and external observances of devotion. We shall always be in a hurry and under a sense of pressure, which will soon lead to disgust and low spirits.

A lack of jealousy of ourselves at times and places of recreation is another source of dissipation. Recreation is itself a dangerous thing; because in one sense it ought to distract and dissipate us, if it is to do us any good; and of such consequence is this distraction, that recreation well-managed is one of the greatest powers of the spiritual life, a fountain of excellent cheerfulness, and a powerful enemy of sins of thought.

A want of jealousy over ourselves at recreation is a cause of dissipation. The same may be said of building castles in the air and of that lax spirit which is always desiring dispensations from little obligations and self-imposed rules. I say self-imposed rules, for why impose them if they are not to be kept, and how can they be kept unless we be more jealous of seeking a dispensation when we ourselves are the dispensing power than when it must be sought from someone else?

The consequences of this dissipation are unfortunately too well-known to all of us to require any long description. First comes self-dissatisfaction, which is the cankerworm of all devotion.

Then captiousness and self-defense, after which we feel that the power to pray is gone from us, as our strength goes from us in an illness. These are followed by positive ill-temper, in an hour of which we lose weeks of struggle and progress. With this is coupled a morbid inclination to judge and criticize others. Or if we have grace to keep down these more gross evils, our dissipation shows its power in multiplying our distractions at prayer, in making us peevish after Communion, or reserved with our director, or in drawing us into an effeminate way of performing our duties, and giving us a great distaste for penance.

The next development of spiritual idleness is sadness and low-spirits. It is no uncommon thing for spiritual persons to speak of sadness as if it were some dignified interior trial, or as if it were something to call out pure sympathy, kindness and commiseration—whereas in by far the greater number of instances it is true to say that no state of the spiritual life represents so much venial sin and unworthy imperfection as this very sadness. It is not humility, for it makes us querulous rather than patient. It is not repentance, for it is rather vexation with self than sorrow for the offense against God. The soul of sadness is self-love. We are sad because we are weary of well-doing and of strict living. The great secret of our cheerfulness was our anxiety and diligence to avoid venial sins, and our ingenious industry to root them out. We have now become negligent on that very point, and therefore we are sad. If indeed we still try, as much as we did before, to avoid actual venial sins, we have lost the courage to keep ourselves away from many pleasant times and places which we know to be to us occasions of venial sin. We content ourselves with an indistinct self-confidence that we shall not fall; and at once the light of God's countenance becomes indistinct also, and the fountain of inward joy ceases to flow. We desire to be praised, and are unhappy if no notice is taken of what we do. We seek publicity as something which will console, rest and satisfy us. We want those we love to know what we are feeling and suffering, or what we are doing and planning. The world is our sunbeam and we come out to bask in it.

No wonder that we are sad! How many are there whose real end in the spiritual life is self-improvement rather than God, and how little they suspect it! Now perhaps it is true to say that we never attain in the way of self-improvement a point which seems to us quite easy of attainment. We are always below the mark we aimed at. Here again is another source of sadness. But whatever way we look at this miserable disposition we shall find that the secret fountain of all its phases is the want of mortification, and more especially of external mortification. In a word, who ever found any spiritual sadness in men trying to be good which did not come either from a want of humility or from habitually acting without distinct reference to God? But the consequences of sadness are of the most fearful description. Nothing gives the devil so much power over us. Mortal sin itself very often gives him less purchase over our souls. It blunts the Sacraments and destroys their influence upon us. It turns all sweet things bitter and makes even the remedies of the spiritual life act as if they were poisons. Under its morbid action we become so tender that we are unable to bear pain, and tremble at the very idea of bodily mortification.

The courage which is so necessary for growth in holiness oozes out of us, and we become timid and passive where we ought to be bold and venturesome. The vision of God is clouded in our soul, and every day the fit of sadness lasts it is carrying us further and further out of our depth, and beyond the reach of rational consolation. It seems a strong thing to say, but it is in reality no exaggeration that spiritual sadness is a tendency toward the state of Cain and Judas. The impenitence of both took root in a sadness which came out of a want of humility, and that want was itself the fruit of acting with a view to self, rather than a view to God.

Above all things we must be careful not to let sadness force us away from our regular Communions, or from any of the strictness we may practice. We must be all the more faithful to them because we are sad; and we must beware of adopting any change while the cloud is on us. Exactness in little duties is a wonderful source of cheerfulness; and set mortifications, few and not severe, but quietly persevered in, will cast out the evil spirit. We must look out for opportunities of giving way to others; for that brings with it softness of heart and a spirit of prayer. We must make the use of our time a subject of particular examination of conscience, and always have on hand some standing book or occupation with which to fill up gaps of vacant time. We must never omit our devotions to our Blessed Lady, whom the Church so sweetly calls "the cause of our joy"; and we must consider that day lost on which we have not thus done homage to her. Finally, we must regard, not the act only which we do, but the time which obedience has fixed for doing it, whether it be the obedience of self, rule, family or director; for the marvelous virtue of obedience resides often more in the time and manner of an act than in the act itself, just as the spiritual life itself consists not so much in an assemblage of certain actions, as in the way in which we do all our actions.

To these two types of idleness, dissipation and sadness, we must add another. It is a kind of sloth, or general languor, which it is very hard to describe, but the main features of which everyone will recognize. Some time has passed since we had a clear view of ourselves. We have got out of sight of ourselves, and are journeying on like men driving in the dark.

Then something occurs which wakes us up to a consciousness of our position. We find that we are continually making resolutions, and as continually breaking them. They form, as usual, part of our morning prayer, and in an hour or two they have passed from our minds as though we had never made them.

Even if we reflect upon them and make some little effort to put them into execution, we find that they are utterly nerveless, and without power or animation. We do not exactly turn a deaf ear to the inspirations which we are receiving at all hours, but we are dilatory in carrying them out, and so the time for them passes by and another duty comes in the way, and it is too late. So that on the whole we hardly correspond to any of our inspirations.

All this is bad enough. But there is added to it a physical feeling of incapacity to make any exertion. It seems to us as if any effort was out of the question; and what is in truth merely a moral malady puts on all the semblance and feeling of a bodily indisposition, and soon causes one. We then begin to make light of serious twinges of conscience, and we are peevish and impatient of any warning or admonition, or of any attempt to bring spiritual matters before us. Everything that everybody does seems inopportune and out of good taste.

Without rhyme or reason, we have an almost universal nausea of men and things, and we give in to "the spirit of causeless irritation" which characterizes the paralytic. It is as if life were worn out and we had got to the end of things, as if we had worked our way through the upper coats of existence down to what Bossuet calls "the inexorable ennui which forms the basis of human life." In this state we are not only distracted at prayer, but slovenly also; and even the Sacraments we treat with a kind of lazy irreverence and formal familiarity, which it is frightening to think of. In fact, our state is a kind of passive possession of the spirit of disgust and sloth; it is as if we had lost the power of being serious, and were numb, or in a trance, so far as spiritual things are concerned. It is this state to which dissipation is always tending; and if we are so unfortunate as not to have checked it in its earlier stages, but find ourselves actually under this oppression, we must rouse ourselves and act with as much vigor as if we had fallen into mortal sin.

But before we conclude the subject of spiritual idleness, we must consider the greatest, the waste of time. The use of time is a large subject; and it is one of far greater consequence than many suppose, in those who are aiming at perfection. Very few faults are irreparable, but the loss of time is one of those few. Now, when we consider how easy a fault it is, how frequent, how silent, how alluring, we shall discern something of its real danger. Idleness when it has fastened upon us, is a perfect tyranny, a slavery whose shackles are felt whatever limb we move, or even when we are lying still. It is also a captivating bondage; whose very sweetness renders it more perilous. But the worst feature about it is its deceitfulness. No idle man believes himself to be idle, except in the lucid intervals of grace. No one will credit how strong the habit of losing time will rapidly become. To break away from it requires a vehemence and a continuity of effort to which few are equal. Meanwhile the debatable land which lies between it and lukewarmness is swiftly traversed. The hourly accumulation of minute carelessness is clogging and hampering the soul, while it is also running us fearfully into debt to the temporal justice of God. It makes our life the very opposite of His. His minute notice of us stands in dreadful contrast with our half-intentional and half-unintentional oblivion and disregard of Him. I doubt if a jealous and conscientious use of time can ever, as many spiritual excellencies can, become a habit. I suspect time is a thing which has to be watched all through life. It is a running stream every ripple of which is freighted with some tell-tale evidence which it hastens to depose with unerring fidelity in that sea which circles the throne of God. It makes us tremble to think of St. Alphonsus just after he had made his solemn vow never to waste a moment of time. We feel that a man who with his humility and discretion dared to commit himself to such a life, could only end by being raised upon the altars of the Church.

It is plain that every one of these types of idleness might be made the subject of a little treatise. Perfection in the world is a difficult affair, and many things are fatal to it. Idleness perhaps slaughters more in the spiritual life than anything else, because it is so very hard for persons in the world not to be idle. Everything around us is pusillanimous and exaggerated. The ideas which pass current are little and low. The air we breathe is languor. The types we behold are pompous follies. Of spiritual romance there is enough, of spiritual foppery more than enough, but of healthy mortification and sincere manly devotion less than would seem possible, if the fact were not certain. Thus, everything draws us to idleness and to inutility. It is a common observation that religious, of both sexes, are strikingly cheerful. This is owing in no slight degree to the preservation from idleness which rule and community life ensure.

We have none of those helps, and therefore we have more to dread from this particular enemy. In fact, the danger and the fatal character of idleness may be reckoned among the prominent characteristics of the attempt to attain perfection in the world. We have already found that for perfection in the world a peculiar exercise of patience is necessary in order to supply the place of a religious rule. So now we must give a more than common attention to the industrious use of time and the discreet management of recreations, in order to meet dangers which religious are beautifully defended from by community life, and a community life invented by a saintly founder. Idleness must be a very prominent object in our warfare, otherwise we shall never attain to the perfection which the Saints tell us is open to people in the world.

CHAPTER 5

REST

The last disposition which makes up our normal state is *rest,* seemingly the very opposite of the fatigue which we addressed previously. But we must not imagine this rest to consist either in a cessation from struggle, or a deliverance from fatigue. This is contrary to the idea of the spiritual life. The rest we are speaking about is a truer rest, a higher rest, a rest of altogether a different kind. It has these five characteristics. First, it is supernatural. Tired nature cannot supply it. It would be no rest at all if it came from any fountain short of Heaven. If it comes from any human heart, it can only be from the Sacred Heart of God made Man. Secondly, it lasts but for a little while at a time. It comes and goes like an angel's visitation. Yet, thirdly, brief as its visit is, its effects are lasting. It refreshes and animates us in a way which no earthly consolation can even imitate, much less rival. It is food in the strength of which we can go all the way to the mountain of God. Fourthly, it is very peaceful. It produces no excitement. It moves away none of our existing devotions or spiritual exercises. It is no disturbing force to our vocation, no overruling impulse to our discretion. And last of all, it unites us to God: and what is that union but a participation of His eternal tranquility, a foretaste of the Sabbath in His paternal lap forevermore?

In trying to draw out for you the varieties of this welcome and beautiful rest, I must caution you not to be cast down if I make it consist in things which seem far above your present attainments. The fact is that these high things are begun in you. It may still be with them their day of small beginnings. Nevertheless, they are begun; and with them comes the gift of rest, to increase as they increase, but to be from the very first a substantial gift of our compassionate Father who is in Heaven.

This divine rest consists first in detachment from creatures. As we grow in holiness our attachments to creatures weaken, and those that remain riveted are riveted in God. It is not that sanctity lies in unfeelingness. Look at St. Francis de Sales stretched on the floor of the room where his mother had just died, and sobbing as if his heart was broken. Strong angels look at the prostrate saint without upbraiding; for his grief is a human holiness rather than a human weakness. Not for a moment, said he, in all that tempest of grief was his will removed one line's breadth from the sweet sovereign will of God. All that is irregular, earthly and inordinate in our attachment fades out. Nay, we are sensibly conscious to ourselves of an actual decay of all strong feelings, of whatever kind, in our hearts. And the absence of these is rest; for strong earthly feelings are a tyranny.

Secondly, we have now no worldly end in view; and thus, there is nothing proximate to disquiet us. What success can we have to look forward to? Is it a point in riches we would fain reach? Or a summit on which an ambitious imagination has often placed us in our daydreams? Or a scheme that we are burning to realize? Such things belong not to the spiritual.

Not even works of mercy now can be ends of themselves, ends in which to rest. They are but stepping-stones we lay down for God's glory and His angels to pass over the earth and bless its misery. There may be rest in straining to a supernatural end, or the very strain may be more welcome than the most luxurious rest. But there can be no rest for those who are straining after a worldly end, blameless even if perchance it be.

Thirdly, holiness brings us rest, because it delivers us even from spiritual ambition, in any of its various forms. The inordinate pursuit of virtue is itself a vice, and the anxious desire to be speedily rid of all our imperfections is a delusion of self-love. To desire supernatural favors is almost a sin; to ask for supernatural tokens is nearly always an indiscretion. Present grace is not only the field of our labor, it is also the haven of our rest. We must trust God and be childlike with Him even in our spiritual progress. We must make a bed of our vileness and a pillow of our imperfections; and nothing can soil us while humility is our rest. Ambition is not the less wrong, nor greediness the less repulsive, because they are spiritual. When God feeds us with His hand, is that a time for eagerness? When spiritual ambition is mortified, not into indifference, but into patience, prayer and calm hope, then there is rest.

One consequence of all these dispositions is a readiness to die; and this is in itself a fourth source of rest. What is there to keep us? Why should we linger on? Dare we pray with St. Martin to stay and work if we are necessary to God's people? Are we so foolish as to dream we have a mission, which is to delay us like Mary after the Ascension, or the Evangelist St. John till the first century was run out? When we are going on a journey, and are not ready, we are all bustle and heat. Preparations have to be made, our last orders given, and our farewells said. But when all is done, and it is not time yet, we sit down and rest. The rooms do not look like home, because we are going, and our attachments are packed up, like the works, merits and forgiven sins of a dying man. If we have any feeling besides that of rest, it is rather impatience. But in a spiritual man impatience to die would be no trifling immortification. Consequently, the readiness to die, without impatience, is rest. The contented animal that stretches itself in the shade of the noonday field does not rest with greater sensible enjoyment than the immortal soul that is bravely detached from mortal things.

It belongs to our nature to incline to rest in ends, and not in means. This opens out to us a fifth source of rest.

For everything is an end, no matter how transient, if only it be referred to God. Indeed, it is an end in a sense in which no merely earthly thing can be so, for it participates in the end of all ends and ultimate rest of all things, God Himself. Hence our very struggle is rest, our very fatigue rest; for they are both made up of countless things each of which is in itself a resting place and an end. Has not everyone felt at times, only too rarely, the joy steal over him that he has no wish or will before him? Nothing is unfulfilled, because God is everywhere. He feels for God and has found Him; and so, he has nothing to seek, nothing to desire. Possible evils are allowed to present themselves to his imagination, only that he may realize more utterly the gladness of his complete indifference to them. He is at rest. Earth has hold of none of his heartstrings. The whole world is full of ends to him. He can lie down anywhere; for everything is a bed, because he refers all things to God. If this kind of rest would sometimes last a little longer—but God knows best. Even the wish would break the deliciousness of that heavenly rest.

Humility furnishes us with the next source of rest. And this in two ways. First of all, it makes us contented, contented with our infirmities, though not contented with ourselves. God forbid this last should ever be! Thus, it makes us content, childlike and calm; and there is rest in the very sound of all those words. Secondly, it brings us rest in another way. For it not only subdues us by keeping us down in the sense of our own nothingness, but it exhilarates us by pouring the pure light of grace around

us and making us feel how entirely we owe everything to
God. Did anyone ever see a humble man with an unquiet
heart? Except when some storm of grief or loss swept over
him, never! Humility is rest, sweet rest and safe, and which
leaves no reproaches or misgivings behind, and it is a rest
within the reach of the lowest of us.

The last source of rest is difficult to describe and we
can only have some idea of it. It is the rest which comes
from the bare thought of God, or rather which is itself the
bare thought of God. Sometimes, in a beautiful climate, we
come upon a scene, which by its surpassing beauty so satisfies mind, heart and senses, that we sit entranced, taking
it in without understanding it, and resting in the simple
enjoyment of the sight. For a while a man may sit amid
the folds of Etna, beneath a shady tree, on the marvelous
mountain shelf of Taormina, and look out upon the scene.
Everything that wood and water, rock and mountain, daz-
zling sky and translucent air can do, with the grand spirit
of old history brooding over all, is there. It cannot be ana-
lyzed or explained. We are taken in the nets of a beauty
which masters us. The sheer thought of it is a joy without thought for hours. This is a poor way of typifying
the rest which is in the glorious, overshadowing thought
of God. It is a self-sufficing rest, not only because He is
almighty, all-holy and all-wise, nor because He is our own
near and fatherly God, but simply and sheerly because He
is God. Words will make it no clearer. God gives it to us
sometimes and we know it; and seen through it, brighter
than Sicilian air, more limpid than Arethusa's fountain, our

struggle and fatigue look fair and delectable in that heavenly medium. But in whatever measure God visits us with this sort of light, true it is that such is the normal state of our spiritual life—struggle and fatigue and not only after these but also during these, there remains a sabbath for the people of God. They rest in the languor of love here, until their rest deepens into His eternal bosom hereafter.

CHAPTER 6

STRUGGLES WITH TEMPTATION

One of the simplest ways to see where we stand is to see how much we are tempted. Temptation is no less a contradiction than knowledge of our spiritual progress. Temptations are the raw material of glory, though they might seem instead a punishment or curse. Managing them is as great a work as the government of an empire, and requires an endless and complete vigilance.

We may be shocked to look upon the world and its ways, and then to think that God became Man and died upon the Cross for its redemption. But we are equally shocked to look at the lives of good men and examine their way of living, and then put one of the maxims of the Gospel alongside of them. At this very hour thousands of souls are earnestly complaining to God of their temptations, and hundreds of confessionals are filled with whispered and impatient complaints of their number and strength. Yet, St. James says, "My brethren, count it all joy when you shall fall in various temptations." It is plain, therefore, that we either do not know or do not always bear in mind the true nature and character of temptations.

There are nearly as many temptations as we have thoughts, and our only victory over them is through persisting courage, and an indomitable spirit of cheerfulness. The arrows of temptation fall harmless and blunted from a joyful heart, which has first of all cast itself so low in its humility that nothing can cast it lower. Be joyous, or, to use Scripture words, "Rejoice, and again I say rejoice," and you will not heed your temptations; neither will they harm you.

Temptations are not sins, although in nine cases out of ten our unhappiness comes from failing to see this. Some defilement seems to come from the touch of a mere temptation; and at the same time, it reveals to us, as nothing else does, our extreme feebleness and constant need of grace—and of very great grace. When temptation presses our fallen and infirm nature, the tenderness is so sensible and so acute that it gives us at once the feeling of a wound or a disease. Yet we must be careful always to distinguish between a sin and a temptation.

Temptations either come from within us, or from a source outside of us, or partly the one and partly the other. Those from within ourselves arise, either from our senses, which are free and undisciplined, or from our passions, which are wild and uncorrected. Temptations from the outside attack us in two ways. In one way, by delighting us, such as riches, honors, attachments and distractions; in the other by attacking us as the demons do. Those which partake of the nature of both possess the attractions of both.

In one sense, however, all temptations consist in an alliance between what is inside of us, and what is outside of us. We must not attribute too much to the devil, nor be without fear of him, or without a true and scriptural estimate of his awful and malignant role. He goes about seeking whom he may devour. He is a roaring lion, when the roar will affright us, and a noiseless serpent when success is to be ensured by secrecy. He has reduced the possibilities and probabilities of our destruction to a science which he applies with the most unrelenting vigor, the most masterly intelligence, almost unfailing power, and with the most ubiquitous variety.

It is never a mere fight between man and the devil. Wherever temptation is, so is God. There is not one which His will has not permitted, and there is not a permission which is not an act of love as well. He has given His whole wisdom to each temptation. He has weighed and measured each by the infirmity of each tempted soul. He has deliberately contemplated the consequences of each, in union with its circumstances, and the least feature has not escaped Him. The most hidden danger has been an element in His judgment. All this while the devil is passive and powerless. He cannot lay a finger on the child until its loving Father has prescribed the exact conditions, and has forewarned the soul by His inspirations, and prepared it in advance with the proportionate relief of grace.

Nothing is at random, as if temptations were hurrying here and there, like wasps in a bad summer. Moreover, each temptation has its own crown prepared for it, if we correspond to grace and are victorious. I do not know any picture of God more affecting, or more fatherly, than the vision of Him which faith gives us than this: His great care and paternal guidance while we are being tempted. "Where were You, Lord, while I was being tempted!?" cried the Saint of the desert. "Close to you. My son, all the while," was the tender reply.

Nevertheless, temptation is refined suffering, above that of sickness and adversity. There is something loathsome in the breath which it breathes upon us, something horribly fascinating in its eye, and paralyzing in its touch. We are faint and sick with the sense of our own corruption and helpless weakness; and the thrilling interests involved in our resisting or succumbing agitate the most inward life of our soul. It is foolish either to deny the suffering or to make light of it. In either case we shall be less able to endure it. It must be in the nearness of God, and in the prompt superfluity of grace, that we must find our cheerfulness and our consolation.

With all his wisdom, the devil is constantly overreaching himself in temptations, not from stupidity, though perhaps God may stupefy him from time to time, but from his ignorance of the grace which has been sent us invisibly. God's love is always so far above either our merits or even our expectations, that neither we nor the tempter can ever come to believe it beforehand. Thus the devil sometimes tempts us too openly, and we are on our guard; or he sends us the wrong kind of temptation, as one man sometimes gets a letter intended for another; or he sends the right temptation at the wrong time; or, as he cannot always read our thoughts, he puts a wrong interpretation on our outward actions; or he leaves off too soon; or he persists too long; or he underestimates the effect of penance and our love of God on the old habits of past sin.

So it is that from one cause or another that he is continually overreaching himself. This is a fact to be dwelt upon. There are many who would answer quite correctly about Satan and the limitations of his power, who nevertheless practically in their own minds entertain a wrong idea of him. They look upon him as God's rival, a sort of wicked god, with godlike attributes all evil, and an omnipotence of iniquity. They do not remember that he is simply our fellow creature, and a conquered and blighted creature. Although we have reason to fear him, still, we are not panic-stricken with the hourly companionship of our own corrupt nature. And we have far more to fear from it than from him.

No matter how great the pain and annoyance that the soul experiences from temptations, it is very often a gift of God not to be delivered from them. Sometimes it is even wise not to pray for deliverance, but only for valor to fight a good fight. St. Paul three times asked to have his thorn removed, in imitation doubtless of Our Lord's triple prayer to have His chalice pass from Him; and the answer which

God gave was a proof how great a gift the temptation, or its permission, really was.

We may be consoled to know that when the devil attacks our body it is often a sign that he has been secretly attacking our soul, and has been foiled. It is also a characteristic of his efforts rather to turn us from virtue than to impel us to vice. This is particularly the case with spiritual people. With them sins of omission make more for him than sins of commission, not only because it is more difficult to lead a spiritual man into to neglect a good rather than commit an evil, but also because sins of commission stir him to repentance. Lukewarmness is often nothing more than a clogging up of the paths of the soul with sins of omission, which hinders the cool and salutary flow of grace.

Nevertheless, the approaches of the devil will hardly ever take the vigilant by surprise. Whether it be of the spiritual nature of our soul, or of the forewarnings of grace, we almost always have a warning of his coming, provided we have a habit of self-recollection. The great thing when we feel that warning is not to be upset, but to meet him in the calmness of humility. This calmness must never desert us during the whole of the fight, least of all when we feel the delight which in many cases the temptation will excite without fail. There are whole classes of temptations which would not be temptations at all were it not for the delight. But the delight is not consent. We are not the masters of the first indeliberate movements of our own hearts and minds. The enemy may run his hand gleefully over the keys before we are aware. But there must be a deliberate acceptance and retention of the delight before it becomes consent, or a sin.

When does temptation strike? It is to be observed that we may often have seasons of great grace, without being at all aware of it, from the extreme hiddenness of the operations of the Holy Spirit in our souls. But temptation is a much more obvious thing than grace, and it is generally the case that a season of peculiar temptation is also a season of peculiar grace. And this it is a consolation to know.

There are also times of temptation when our own past sin, or our present culpable inadvertence, is their cause. We have brought them upon ourselves, and this makes them all the harder for our self-love to bear. Disturbance forms no part of accepted penance. Times of prayer are also times of peculiar temptation. This was naturally to be expected, inasmuch as there is nothing the devil so much desires to interrupt as our communication with God. Indeed, the access and force of temptations forms a part of the supernatural difficulties of prayer.

The spiritual life itself, with its times of retreat or of increased recollection, brings us into periods of peculiar temptation. The world with its outward attractions is removed from us, and the devil, in dread of these epochs of recollection, more than supplies their place with the inward application of temptation. There are times also when he teases us with temptations to which he knows beforehand that we shall not yield, because they disturb us, or dishearten us, or throw us into a general irritability.

There are other times in which he tempts us in the grace we have just used to overcome him, and in the strength of which we actually have overcome him. The reason for this is that our success has thrown us off our guard, and we never dream of failing in a virtue which but a moment before has filled us with the joy of victory. Thus, when Our Lord put His confidence in His Father, the devil first tempted Him by it.

There are many kinds of temptation. Some temptations are frequent; and there is a peculiar danger in their frequency. They weaken us and break up the calm of our recollection, or they tire us, and at last we sit down and give up the battle out of weariness, or we get used to them, and lose our proper fear of them. Generally, frequent temptations of this sort have some connection with our ruling passion.

Some temptations are durable, and they also have dangers of their own and consolations of their own. Their chief danger is their outliving our powers of perseverance, whereas their chief consolation is that their very durability is a sign they have not triumphed. The pressure is removed the moment we consent, and consequently the lasting of the burden is a measure of the grace God has given us to resist it. Although Jesus seems fast asleep in the boat, the fact that it is not submerged in the rough waters is because He is there.

But what are the uses of temptations? So many and so great that I can do no more than indicate a few of them here. They try us, and we are worth nothing if we are not tried. Our trial is the one thing God cares for, and it is the only thing which gives us the least knowledge of ourselves.

Temptations disgust us with the world almost as effectually as the sweetnesses which God gives us in prayer. For all that, how hard it is to become truly disgusted with the world, and how very much more we really love the world than we have any idea of! What price should anything be which helps us to a true and final divorce from this seductive world!

Temptations enable us to merit more, that is, they increase God's love of us, and our love of God, and our glory with God hereafter. They punish us for past sins; and we ought to court such punishments eagerly, for five minutes of free-will suffering on earth are worth five years of the tardy cruelties of Purgatory. They purify us for God's presence, which is the very office of Purgatory itself, and anticipate its work and so prevent its fires. They prepare us for spiritual consolations and perhaps, they even earn them for us. St. Philip says that God gives us first a dark and then a bright day all through life. Are not souls whom He has touched obliged to hold their tongues, because they have no words to express the happiness it is? Yet without the temptation, the consolation probably never would have come.

Temptations teach us our own weakness, and so humble us; and could our guardian angels do more than this for us, in all the variety of their affectionate care over us? Dear Prince, more than brother! I say it not in light esteem of his unutterable kindness, who never leaves me a solitary speck in this huge creation of God, and whose services I shall never know till they all meet me at the doom brighter than a thousand suns, and whose love will come to a head rather than to an end when he embraces me in the first moment of the resurrection of the flesh! But he wishes nothing so much as to keep me humble, and temptations help him to do the work.

How shallow would all spirituality be if it were not for temptations. How shallow good men actually are, who are not much tempted! The Church can never trust them in her hour of need. They are always on the side on which St. Thomas Beckett would not have been. Temptations again make us more watchful; instead of leading into sin, they hinder the shallow bank of sins. They make us more fervent, kindling in us a fire of love so great that it burns away the hay and straw of venial sin, and cauterizes the half-healed wounds which mortal sin has made. A transport of generous love can do a work as great, and the great work as well, as a year's fast on bread and water, with a discipline a day.

Lastly, they teach us spiritual knowledge. What we know of self, of the world, of the demons and of the artifices of divine grace, is chiefly from the phenomena of temptation, and from our defeats quite as much as from our victories.

These are the uses of temptations, and they leave seven permanent blessings behind them. They leave us merit, which is no transient thing. It has vitality that when mortal sin has put it to death, penance can bring it to life again. They leave us love, both God's love of us and our love of Him. They leave us humility, and with that all other gifts of God. The Holy Spirit Himself rests upon the humble, and makes His dwelling in their hearts. They leave us solidity. Our building is so much higher than it was, and its foundations more safely and more permanently settled. They leave us self-knowledge, without which all we do is done in the dark, and the sun never shines upon the soul, nor is the ground ever clear for the operations of grace. They leave us with our self-love killed. Does life have a fairer task than the burial of its worst and most odious enemy? Its dead body is more to us than the relic of an apostle, and surely that is saying much. They leave us thrown upon God. For no nurse ever put a babe into its father's arms more carefully or more securely than temptations put us into the extended arms of God. And yet we complain—complain of our temptations! Perverse fallen nature! It has always been so; from beneath the apple tree in Eden to this hour, we do not know our own happiness, and in our ignorance, we pick a fight with it!

People often run into something like Manicheism, and end up with an idea of Almighty God which has drifted widely from what Scripture teaches. We forget that the devil is only one of three enemies against whom we vowed to do battle at Baptism, and thus we transfer to him all the phenomena which belong rather to the flesh and the world. The same secret vanity which leads us to a superstitious view of grace, as a talisman which is to act without the cooperation of our own resolute will, is the source of these false views of the devil's activity. It breaks the shame of our falls to believe that in every instance we have wrestled and been thrown by an evil angel of tremendous power, and not that through cowardice, effeminacy and self-love we have simply given in to the suggestions of our own irresolute will.

It is rather the case that in certain temptations men will allow themselves to be almost passive, from this horrible doctrine about the devil. Were they logical, they would soon come to believe that the idea of the necessity of sin is positively blasphemous. What their view really amounts to is this, that man is a certain organized reasonable instrument, who is possessed by the devil, and that God comes and tries to establish a counter-possession by means of faith, grace and Sacraments, and that man has little to do with the matter except to consent to be the battlefield of the two spiritual powers. Everyone shudders when it is put into these words. But follow a soul who has got this wrong idea into the whole region of temptations, and you will see what mistakes it makes and what misfortunes it encounters, and how at last, to use St. Bernard's figure, it needs no devil to tempt it, because it is a devil to itself.

Further, mistakes can be made about temptations themselves as about everything else in the spiritual life, and we have already implied and explained many in what has been said. Now, there are four particular mistakes on which a few words may be of use.

The first mistake is that we are apt to think the time spent in combating temptations is time lost. We are all very much at peace, and more or less consciously in the presence of God, during our ordinary occupations. Then, the time comes for visiting the Blessed Sacrament, and all at once we are assailed with a multiplicity of temptations. We have but a quarter of an hour to be there, and the whole time has gone in doing battle with these miserable temptations. Or again, we rise in the morning, full of the thought of God, and say prayers while we are dressing. We then kneel down and begin our meditation, and a host of temptations assail us right away. The time passes, and what have we done? Nothing but fight these temptations, and it seems as though we did not fight well enough!

Here we must remember that we are not to serve God for consolations, or after our own fashion, and according to our own taste; but according to His wisdom and His will. His rewards are not attached to the good works we prescribe to ourselves, but to the combats in which it is His good pleasure to involve us. Time is only lost when we do not do the will of God. What is our object? It is either to be glorifying God, or to be perfect, or to reach Heaven. Fighting a temptation is the shortest road to all these three ends.

The second mistake is the misconception of temptations by negligent souls. Sometimes they think it a mark of spiritual advancement to be inactive and almost passive under temptations. They apply to themselves advices which belong only to the perfect, or maxims which were intended for the scrupulous. In this way, they fall into a pernicious habit of letting dangerous thoughts pass through their minds without scrutiny. This not only weakens their mind, but seems to saturate it with undesirable images and inclinations. Their feeling about sin ceases to be what it was, and their confidence in themselves increases as the probabilities of a fall increase also.

The consequence of all this is a state of inaction and of general slovenliness with God, from which, if they are roused at all, it is probably by the commission of mortal sin. Lukewarm souls have sometimes been renewed to holiness in this dreadful way, and God has shown them mercy even in the judicial chastisement of this adorable permission. But it is a process, the very thought of which should make us shudder, and which probably never happened to anyone who was negligent because he trusted to repentance willfully delayed, and to the uncertain possibilities of an eventual reconciliation with God. Whoever has familiarized himself with what he knows are temptations, and has domesticated the thought of them in his mind, no matter of what class they may be, has taken a decided step toward that state of tepidity whose logical development is final impenitence.

The third mistake concerns our use of the calms which come between the storms of periodical temptations. Everyone knows by his own experience that he is subject to particular kinds, or to one particular kind of temptations, which come around in perfect hurricanes, like circular storms with fair and tranquil weather between. We have been going on in our ordinary way. We see no reason for a change, either in ourselves or in external circumstances, when all at once the storm is down upon us, with the same sort of panic the pagans felt when it thundered out of a clear sky. We are possessed with the images of the temptation. Every outward object turns into them. We are sunk, overhead, deep down, in temptations, and the masterful current is sweeping in eddies above us. It is not as with Peter that a hand was held out as we were in the act of sinking. We are sunk. Yes! and Jesus is with us in the deep where we are.

Now in the storm we have simply nothing to do but to hold fast to God with all our might and main. There is no help for it. It is a mistake to look upon these calms as a time of rest when we may give ourselves up to the simple enjoyment of the absence of the temptations, or of the spiritual sweetness with which these tempests are commonly followed. We must lay our plans then, and make our resolutions, with a foresight of what we have to encounter. We must fix on occasions to avoid, increase our mortifications, and redouble our prayers. If we have gone down in many a storm, it has been because we made holidays of our calms. Remember, in the spiritual life school has a few recesses, while the home afterwards is eternal.

A fourth mistake is the delusion with which the devil tries to possess us, that if we give way in some of the circumstances of the temptation, or to the temptation itself short of sin, we shall weaken it. It is strange that so gross a snare should ever succeed; yet it does so in many cases. We must remember that to yield is to weaken *ourselves*, not the temptation. We shall get no foothold so strong as our first; and men often discover to their cost that even a change of position, without abandoning an attitude of defense, is as good as a defeat in the time of temptation.

How are we to overcome temptations? Cheerfulness is the first thing, cheerfulness the second and cheerfulness the third. The devil is chained. He can bark, but he cannot bite, unless we go up to him and let him do so. We must be of good courage. The power of temptation is in the fainting of our own hearts.

Confidence in God is another spiritual weapon, the more potent because no one can have confidence in God who has not the fullest modesty in regard to himself. God's cause is ours; for temptation is more really the devil's wrath against God who has punished him, than against us, whom he only envies. Our ruin is important to him only as it is a blow at God's glory. God is bound to us, as it were, seeing that it is for His sake that we are thus persecuted. We may be sure, indeed we know infallibly, that we shall never be tried beyond our strength. Prayer, especially earnest vocal prayer, is another obvious means of victory, together with mortification and the frequenting of the Sacraments, which are all wells of supernatural fortitude.

Examination of conscience must help us to detect the weak and vulnerable parts of our nature; and then we must exercise ourselves in acts contrary not only to our peculiar infirmities, but also to our chief temptations. We must avoid idleness, and crush its beginnings. We must not speak of our temptations indiscriminately to persons who have no right to know anything about them, nor even to our spiritual friends. It gives no real relief, and it feeds the ideas. Neither must we be cast down if our director treats our temptations more lightly than we think they deserve. What is the good of speaking to him at all about them, if we are not going to obey his rules and adopt his view and follow his advice?

In times of temptation we must be very careful not to reduce any of our spiritual exercises, a line of conduct for which the evil one may suggest very specious reasons. We have need of all our strength at that moment; and we never know to which of our ordinary exercises God attaches His grace. It would have been better for the Apostles to have struggled through a drowsy, dry, distracted prayer, than to have simply gone to sleep in the Garden of Gethsemane. We must remember also that all our spiritual exercises are less prompt and pleasant when we are under temptations, because we are teased and puzzled by them. Hence nature is more likely to suggest the abridgment or discontinuance of some of them, on the ground of their being useless and spiritless. But although things are established by the mouth of two witnesses, those two must not be the devil and the human spirit.

We must also be cautious not to change our purposes at such times. It is not a time for us to see God's will about changes and vocations. His will just then is that we resist the evil, and therefore that is the single thing for us to do. Furthermore, we must beware even of any new good which makes its appearance, knocks at the door of our heart, or puts itself ready-made into our hands, at such a season. St. Ignatius long since warned us of a family of temptations which present themselves in the disguise of good. God would not send us the good then, or in that way. His will, once more, is that we should resist the evil. The good will keep, if it be really good; and He will send us peaceable times when we can calmly and deliberately take it upon ourselves.

We must also be upon our guard against very little temptations, or such as we should call little. For things must have comparative magnitudes, even where our souls are concerned. It is no uncommon thing for a man who has resisted great temptations to fall in little ones. This is very understandable. Wherever there is dignity in an action or a suffering we can the better brace ourselves up to it; for we can draw largely upon nature as well as grace. Self-love likes dignity, and will go through endless pain, as if it were an insensible thing, in order to obtain it.

Hence comes the importance of little things in religion. Nature has less to do with them, and so they rivet our union with God more closely. The conversion of souls, works of mercy on a grand scale, visiting prisons, preaching, hearing confessions and even establishing religious institutes, are comparatively easy works when put by the side of exactitude in daily duties, observation of petty rules, minute custody of the senses, kind words and modest exterior which preach the presence of God. We gain more supernatural glory in little things, because more fortitude is required, as they are continuous, uninterrupted and with no dignity about them to spur us on.

Our spirit is more effectually taken captive in little things. Its defeats are more frequent. The very continuity of the actions forms a linked chain, which extends to many things. No attachment is merely natural, no word unaccounted, no step precipitate, no pleasure enjoyed sensually, no joy to evaporate in dissipation, the heart never to rest on fleshly tenderness alone, no action to have its spring in self-will. Then, again, there is something so humbling and secret in little things. Who knows if we count our words, or what feelings we are curbing? God will let us fall in these very respects to hide us more in Himself, and from the eyes of men. We carry the mortification of Jesus about us unseen. It is a slow martyrdom of love. God is the only spectator of our agony. We ourselves find it hard to realize that we are doing such a multitude of trivial things purely for God; hence we have no room for vainglory, no fallacious support of conscious human rectitude.

But in these little things we not only gain more glory for ourselves, rather, we give more glory to God. We show more esteem for Him in them. There must necessarily be a purer motive and sheer faith in little than in great things. Great things by their greatness often hide God, and at the best the esteem in great things is mostly divided between God and the glory of the action, and so the whole work is tainted. Whereas the littleness and baseness of small things, their apparent facility and men's contempt for them, leave the soul face to face with God in the disenchanting twilight of interior mortification. But it is not merely esteem. More actual tribute is paid to God in little things. In great things we have more help given us, and we give God less because we have to labor less. The abundance of grace, the sweetness of it and the animation of spirit from the pursuit of a great object, are three things which lessen our own labor. Yet it is our own toil that is the real tribute to God, just as dry prayers are more meritorious than sweet ones. In great things too we seldom have the liberty of acting as we please. In little ones we have, and we pay that liberty away hour by hour to God as a tribute of fidelity and love.

But esteem and tribute are not all. We sacrifice more to God in little things. We think little of little things, and so we make the sacrifice, not in swelling thoughts of mightiness, but out of a subdued feeling of our own utter nothingness, and of the immensity of our being allowed to make any sacrifice to God at all. We also seek God only, and put aside the pursuit of praise and self. We forego also the enjoyment of strenuous manly action; for what manliness, as men count things, is there in regularity, littleness, exactness and obscurity? Yet this is the only road to solid virtue. It was not what we read of in the Saints that made them saints: it was what we do not read of them that enabled us to wonder at them while we read their lives. Words cannot tell the abhorrence nature has of the piecemeal captivity of little constraints. And as to little temptations, I can readily conceive a man having the grace to be roasted over a slow fire for our dearest Mother's Immaculate Conception or the Pope's supremacy, who would not have the grace to keep his temper in a theological conversation on either of those points of the Catholic Faith.

CHAPTER 7

SCRUPLES

Our next step to gain a right view of ourselves must be to examine more of the symptoms that reveal what is not right with us. First, we may notice great difficulty in resisting temptations, which results in a lack of fidelity to our devotional life. Then we are unable to manage sudden changes, our exterior duties, or control our moods according to the interior life. Then we realize that we have a deficiency of grace. Our examinations of conscience seem like going through the motions, and the inclination to scruples grows within us, as we seem to lose the sight of God which we had before. What could it be? We begin to scrutinize all of our actions, and place the blame on imperfectly fulfilling this or that duty, having this slight attachment to sin in this action, or, that we had this failure on this occasion. Surely that was it! Then, little by little, instead of knowing and repairing our faults we place the blame on this or that incidental detail, and fall more and more into scruples. But this only takes us further from the right view of our sins.

Unlike temptations, scruples do not, or at least very rarely, yield any benefits. A scrupulous man teases God, irritates his neighbor, torments himself and oppresses his director. It would require a whole volume to prove these four infallible propositions; the reader must, therefore, either take them on faith—or make the acquaintance of a scrupulous man.

Everyone who is in trouble and disgrace deserves our empathy. Yet, we have much less pity when the sufferer has no one to blame but himself, and it well-nigh departs altogether when he remains in his suffering of his own obstinate will. Now this is the case with scrupulous persons during all the earlier stages of their trouble, before they become incurable. They are the opprobrium of spiritual physicians, and their cure so intensely difficult that God has sometimes allowed those who were hereafter to be the guides of souls to pass through a supernatural state of scruples, that they might be the better able to minister to the disease in others.

It is a great part of the science of the spiritual life to know a temptation from a sin; and a scruple may almost be defined to be the culpable ignorance of this. Another man may discern that my scruple is not a sin. Yet, if I discerned it for myself, it would not be a scruple, and if I took it on faith when my director told me, I should not be a scrupulous man. This lets us into the secret of the malice of scruples. They are not sins, but they are so full of wrong dispositions that they can become sins at a moment's notice, as well as sources of many sins under the pretext of good. They are little centers of spiritual viruses budding in the soul, a kind of moral flesh-eating bacteria.

It is unfortunate that scrupulous persons are always spoken of with great compassion, far more than they deserve. They elevate their scruples to an interior trial of the soul— which they seldom are. It is unfortunate also that in common conversation the word scruple is often used in a good sense, as if it were something respectable. It would be a great thing if men could get well into their minds this ascetical truth, that there is nothing respectable about a scruple.

A scruple, unlike a temptation, has no intellectual worth. It merits no moral esteem. It does not have the faintest element of spiritual good in it. It is simply a perversity and a wrongness, deserving of pity certainly, but of the same kind that we have for a man who is going to be hanged. Francesca of Pampeluna saw many souls in Purgatory only for scruples; and when this surprised her, Our Lord told her there never was a scruple which was wholly without sin. Scruples are not only bad in themselves; they also give rise to endless mischief. One of the most provoking of them is that men are often deterred from the pursuit of perfection and the constraints of the interior life by the fear of scruples.

A scruple is defined in theology to be a vain fear of sin where there is no reason nor reasonable ground for suspecting sin. Moreover, it is sometimes explained in etymology to mean a stone in a man's shoe which makes him walk lame, and wounds him at every step, which is not an inapt figure for expressing its consequences in the spiritual life. We may also compare a scrupulous man to a horse frightened by shadows to the extent that it makes little progress, backing, disobeying the rein, and often endangering the rider, and when not doing this, then trying his temper. Moreover, he runs into real sin from being frightened by the shadow of imaginary sin. All this is so connected with pride that the tender St. Philip Neri had no mercy on scrupulous persons who would not pay blind obedience to the rules given them. Thus, scruples are quite distinct from delicacy of conscience, which is known not only by its being reasonable, but much more by its being peaceful. Neither is a scruple the same thing as laxity though it is almost worse.

The first item for us to consider regards the causes of scruples. These are three: God, the devil, and ourselves, or the human spirit. In the case of the last, the body contributes, as well as the soul.

First, then, scruples may be from God. These are what I have called supernatural scruples. God may permit us to fall into them for various reasons. Sometimes it is to prepare us for the office of directing souls, in which it is important that we should have an experience of scruples, so as to guide others safely through them.

Sometimes it is as an exterior trial, or what mystics call a dark night of the soul. On the one hand, the use is to wean us from an excessive attachment to spiritual sweetnesses and the extraordinary favors of God, and on the other to let us have our Purgatory on earth. Or, it may be to destroy the lingering activity of self-love. He thus cleanses us from our past faults by a most apt, yet extremely severe penance, confirms us in a salutary fear, and humbles us in the very matters wherein humiliation is felt most distressingly. His share in the process is simply the withdrawing of the gratuitous light in which He allowed the soul to walk before. It was under this subtraction that St. Bonaventure would not say Mass and St. Ignatius refused to eat, that Ippolito Galantini was swallowed up in a sea of scruples, that St. Lutgarde said her office so many times over that God sent an angel to forbid her, and that St. Augustine, as he tells us in his *Confessions,* was so teased with scruples about his natural pleasure in eating and drinking.

Secondly, scruples may be from the devil, who is a positive cause of them, whereas God can never be. Their persuasions and importunities can actually bring it to pass that what is a very little sin, or no sin at all, may be turned into a mortal sin. The devil's object is always real sin. He knows well that scruples are a roundabout road to it, though no less of a sure path for being so.

But thirdly, the greatest fountain of these pathetic and unworthy matters is in ourselves. It is partly in our soul, and partly in our body. This is the most practical part of our subject, and must be considered at greater length. The causes of scruples from our soul are either intrinsic or extrinsic. The intrinsic are five in number.

The first is the want of discernment in temptations, so that a man does not distinguish between temptation and consent. It is difficult to exaggerate its importance, as so many things are vitiated by this unhappy ignorance.

The second is a hidden pride, which takes the shape of self-opinionatedness. There are few men who have not some pet opinions to which they cling with an unreasonable tenacity. They may be very humble in other matters. They may even have a certain amount of intellectual humility. But they cannot be made to discern the exorbitance of their tenacity. If it be on a question of theology, ten to one it becomes implicit heresy in a short time. They cannot see the force of any arguments on the other side. They gullably interpret in their own favor the plainest counter-statements in theologians, whose authority they dare not call in question. From conversations they retire with exactly opposite impression of the other person's opinion from what was meant. Is there any subject on theology which we can never discuss without either sadness or irritability? We may be sure we have got hold of a wrong opinion about it. When this tenacity of judgment fastens upon a question of the spiritual life, it becomes a source of scruples, and a source which is itself poisoned by wrong dispositions. Out of this came Jansenism and

Quietism,[1] and in the secret of private and even conventual life it is, as great writers tell us, unceasingly destroying souls. Safe and happy is the man, if it is possible, and how happy his guardian angel, who, has an opinion outside the limits of the Catholic Faith and the approval of the Church which he would not abandon within ten minutes!

The third cause of scruples is an excessive fear of God's justice or a distrust of His mercy; for it may take either of these forms. If a man has laid to heart what has been said before of looking on God as a Father, he will escape this snare.

It is not that scruples have any real worship of the Divine Justice, but incorrect views of Divine Mercy. Scruples have nothing to do with God for His own sake. There is no devotional spirit about them, nor even a mistaken one. The disguise may be varied almost infinitely, but it is always self-love which is beneath the veil. It is our fear, not God's honor, which leads us to exaggerate the one attribute and to depreciate the other.

The fourth cause is an inordinate anxiety to avoid even the appearance of sin, and to have a full certainty that such and such acts are not sins. We are impatient of the uncertainty in which it has pleased God that we should

---

1 - Editor's note: *Jansenism* is a heresy that denied free will in the reception and use of grace and denied that attrition (imperfect sorrow for sin) was capable of salvation, arguing instead that perfect contrition was necessary. *Quietism* was a heresy that denied free will inasmuch as the soul was annihilated and absorbed into the Divine Essence, even during the present life.

often walk. We would rather change the assurance of faith for the evidence of sight, or the conviction of reason. God has made faith the light of life. We wish for a light more undeniable and brighter. He who loves God wishes to avoid sin; but to wish to avoid the appearance of sin is by no means an infallible proof of sanctity and love. Short of scandal, the Saints have seen almost a shelter in the semblance of sin. It is sin, and not the appearance of it, which wounds God's honor.

The fifth cause is an indiscreet austerity, which shows itself in avoiding the company of others, as if perfection consisted in being morose. There are very few souls which can bear solitude. For the most part it makes them a prey to sin instead of deepening the habit of the presence of God. Hence it was that the old monks of the desert were so reluctant to permit the vocation of those who thought themselves called to the hermit's life. With people in the world the same principles are at work in their measure. To shun society and shut ourselves up, as if to keep out of the way of sin, to avoid rash judgments, to do penance and to practice prayer, is a line of conduct which rarely answers. It is beset with temptations, and an atmosphere of delusions is spread all over it.

When the causes of scruples are in the soul, but are so in consequence of external circumstances, they come either from the permission of God or the temptation of Satan, both of which we have already considered, or from conversing with scrupulous persons, or reading books of spirituality and moral theology which a prudent director would have prohibited us from reading. These two last causes explain themselves, and need no further comment.

The signs of scruples may be inferred from their causes. The first is pertinacity of will and way. It is very rare indeed that a docile man is scrupulous, and when he is so, his scruples are, for the most part, supernatural, and therefore sanctifying. Disobedience is the counterpart of scrupulosity. Pertinacity is the opposite of the spirit of Jesus.

The second sign is a greedy desire to know our own interior state. This comes to pass when self-love entirely possesses us, as if it were a living demon. We must know whether we are in a state of grace. We will not go a step further unless we do know. We must be told whether the sin we have confessed be grave or not. We remain silent until our confessor has told us. God must give us a mathematical certainty in moral questions, or we shall feint. We will give up holiness. We will not try to persevere. So, because we will have more light than God's light, we walk in the darkness, and off a cliff. Our first step is in confusion, our second in cowardice, our third in sadness, and our fourth in irremediable perdition.

The third sign is a frequent change of our opinion for reasons of no importance, together with an inconstancy and anxiety in action. We are disquieted and agitated by fear, even while we persist in caressing it. If we are asked whether there be sin in such or such an action, we answer that there is not. Yet we are frightened of acting even on the conviction of our own reason, coupled with the admonitions of obedience; as if forsooth our soul were worth so much more than the souls of others.

The fourth sign is feeding ourselves with extravagant reflections on the most trivial circumstances of our actions. It belongs to the perverse genius of scruples to give its attention to what is unimportant, and to withdraw it from what is truly important. In other words, it is an essentially impertinent spirit, in the etymological sense of the word. It is always busy, but never at its own business; always at work, but its work is one of confusion, not of order. It hovers among the flowers, lights upon them, turns their cups topsy-turvy, and empties them of their crystal dew, but gets honey out of none of them.

The fifth sign is a fear of sin even in actions which a man perceives to be undeniably excellent. There is something amazing in the stupid ingenuity with which the mind tries to make out a case against good works, and something still more amazing in the power it has of believing in itself, a belief which is not shaken in the slightest by the manifest disbelief of the whole world besides. Occasionally it makes us suspect that there is truth in what someone said, that all men were crazy, and that what we agree to call insanity is only a question of degree. It is useless to argue with men in this disposition—our duty is to command them; our temptation is to strike them.

The sixth sign is a habit of bodily attitudes, postures, gestures, struggles, half-aloud devout reflections, fidgets, inability to sit still, which an old Benedictine writer calls simply ridiculous, but which modem manners would rather deem distressing. I suppose the meaning of this is that the disease of the soul has spread out and transferred itself into the organization, and has now reached the feet and finger-tips. This can only be cured as we cure children who rub their eyes and bite their nails, whether those practices come of idleness, eagerness, temper, or abstraction.

The seventh sign is a perpetual revisiting of our past confessions, a wish to rake them up and overhaul them, and see if we cannot find matter for some choice scruple in them. We do not know what is wrong about them. We even shrink from specifying, lest the charm should go. But it is a delightful misery, a wretchedness in which a scrupulous spirit revels.

The scrupulous man is dying to make a fresh general confession, but not at all inclined to take any great pains to prepare for it, or any vigorous measures against present faults. But it establishes his control over the director. He triumphs over his reluctance and goes to it infallibly sure of one thing, that what he mistakenly conceives to be the principal sin is just that one sin, thank God, which does not beset us. Anything but that. Certainly not that. And all this while we fancy that being in motion is necessarily progress. Alas! we are like the sails of a windmill, always on the move, but only round and round.

Just the same, the signs and developments of scruples are somewhat different, according to the causes from which they proceed, and it is very important to notice this phenomenon. For example, when the scruples arise from our own temperament, they are generally the same.

They lack variety, because pertinacity sticks to the same things, and somber thoughts turn away from change. In this way, we never get out of the identical round which we have paced before, grinding the same clay, to make the same bricks.

When, however, our scruples proceed from the devil, the case is rather different. Then they are quite numerous and extremely variable. They are for the most part very dishonorable to God, and fasten by preference either on one of His ever-blessed attributes, or on the sweet mystery of the Incarnation, or on the Sacraments. They are accompanied by a special darkening of the mind, a sort of eclipse of faith, which is a favorite resort of the evil one. We are numb and cold in prayer, oppressed with an enervating languor, and desire exceedingly to relax our rule of life, at least for a while.

If our scruples are from God, they cease periodically, and cease all at once. This is an infallible sign of their being from God. It would not happen naturally. The natural laying aside of a scrupulous conscience cannot be instantaneous and complete. Another mark of divine scruples is that we go on toward perfection in spite of them, or rather secretly because of them. The more they tease us the more constant we are in our spiritual exercises, the more gentle and forbearing with others, the more obedient to our guides and superiors. We will look to God the more smilingly with all the plenitude of a filial confidence, while at the same time free of servile dread or of presuming familiarity.

Yet, with all scruples which are not supernatural simply turn on two hinges, ignorance and pusillanimity. Let us do away with the first and fortify the second, and these miserable emissaries of evil cannot harm us.

If we cast an eye upon the subjects on which scruples fasten, we shall see still greater reason to turn from them with mingled repugnance and contempt. First of all, there is prayer. In an unhealthy state of mind, it seems positively to attract scruples to itself. There is no part of it, whether mental, vocal, or spontaneous, nor any considerations, affections, or resolutions, which do not seem to be their favorite food, and from which they receive nothing of the divine life. The Sacraments, especially Confession and Communion, they haunt with a pertinacity only equaled by their versatility.

The dry Communion has its own family of scruples; the fervent Communion another. With one man's confession it is the penance they settle on, with another's the contrition, with another's the narration, with another's the preparation. They're all an equal problem to them, for they taint wherever they touch. The keen air which breathes round the heights on which vows are placed does not impede the respiration of scruples. They are little creatures, but robust, and vows are fine game and glorious food for them. Nothing is higher than a vow, and that is not too high for them. Nothing is lower than a fear of bodily discomfort, and that is not too low for them. Scruples like this are universal insects, and ubiquitous, worse than those teased St. Augustine into being a Manichean in his youth.

Fraternal correction is a perfect luxury to them. It lies in the shade, and there is no strong light upon it, so that it is hard to see the scruple, to be sure of it, and to get a good aim at it. The motives of actions are their favorite hiding places. Temptations are their task.

From the subjects let us pass to the effects of scruples. They are three: blindness, indevotion and laxity. If scruples proceed from ignorance, they also increase and deepen it. They so perturb the mind that all spiritual discernment is impossible. They confuse the boundaries of right and wrong. They remove the ancient landmarks between temptation and sin, between delight and consent. They ravel mortal and venial sin inextricably and indissolubly together. They turn precepts into counsels, and counsels into precepts. They call things by their wrong names, and incur the Prophet's woe of putting bitter for sweet and sweet for bitter. The blind can neither lead the blind, nor walk safely on his own road. The spiritual life is brought to a halt, which must be final unless we can break through the enemy's lines. Scruples must be anathematized in every possible shape, just as a heresy in doctrine, a lawlessness in discipline and a corruption in morals.

The second effect of scruples is indevotion. This is as much as saying that the death of devotion is unfavorable to devotion. But how is it that they kill devotion? Devotion is peace, and they are trouble. Devotion is single-minded, and they are legion. Devotion is docile, and they are disobedience. Devotion worships God, and they worship self. Devotion lives on holy food, and their life is sustained by corrupting the food on which it lives. They prevent the light of prayer from entering our perturbed minds. They interrupt the operations of the Sacraments, and even make them prisoners. They obscure our faith, weaken our hope and relax our charity. They have all the bad effects of temptations without any of the good ones.

The third effect of scruples is laxity. Was any man ever known to be scrupulous in one thing who was not lax in another? The laxest of men are scrupulous men. It is very natural. In the first place, we feel as if we had only a certain amount of conscientiousness, and as we have expended more than was due on one thing, we have all the less left for another. Scruples are a tyranny and an oppression; and submission has its reactions. These drive us to seek consolations in worldly pleasures and natural affections, in all that is bright, beautiful and tender round about us.

Not knowing one thing from another, we strain at gnats and swallow camels. If we have gone wrong by indiscretion in austerities, now we are more wrong by being over our head and ears in comforts. A man who has no spiritual pleasures will compensate himself by the abundance of his bodily enjoyments. And what is all this but laxity? And it is the scruples which the devil causes that mostly set this way.

The remedies for scruples find their place naturally after the consideration of the causes, signs, subjects and effects of scruples. As the want of light is the chief cause of the disease, prayer is one of its principal remedies. We should meditate on cheering subjects, and cultivate a filial devotion to Our Blessed Lady. We must avoid idleness, and prepare ourselves to bodily mortification. We must not easily change our director, or consult many persons, which is the way with light-minded men and shallow spiritualists. Nor should we talk much with scrupulous persons, since the complaint is catching. We must never reflect on our own scruples, but act as we see other good people act, remembering that God is our Father, and the Church a kind mother. The precepts of God and the Church were not meant to take away from us all spiritual sweetness, as the excessive interpretations of the scrupulous and timid would make them do; neither did the Church ever intend by her commands to oblige any man to drive himself mad.

The Commandments of God and the Precepts of the Church, and the reverence of the Sacraments, are in much safer keeping in the hands of a mild theologian than of a stern one, though of course all principles have their extremes and all exaggerations are wrong. But one remedy is as near a specific as anything can be called a specific which does not cure an incurable disease, but restores a man to a passable neurotic kind of spiritual existence. And that is blind obedience. The word explains itself. St. Philip says that scruples may make a truce with a man, when once they have beset him, but a peace never. If we have been once scrupulous, and our scruples have not been from God, we shall carry at the least the weakness of them and nervousness of them to the grave, to receive their final elimination in Purgatory. But blind obedience will cure us to all intents and purposes.

Still, how shall we know that we are really obedient? O most scrupulous of questions! But it shall be answered kindly, though briefly. By these three signs: When you never say, "Oh, but my director is not a saint," or, "I would obey if I was scrupulous and if this were a scruple," or, "I would obey if I could explain myself to my confessor, so that he could really understand my case."

However much there may be of their own fault in what they are now suffering, nevertheless the reality of their suffering entitles them to certain privileges. These privileges however are not only rights, they are also obligations.

The first privilege of scrupulous persons is, that provided they are so instructed by their spiritual guide, it is allowable for them to act even with the fear of sinning while they act. They are bound to do so. If they refuse, they willfully commit five separate faults, which approach more or less near to the confines of venial sin, and not seldom overstep it. These are that they presumptuously set up their own opinion against that of their director, which is pride and obstinacy. They refuse him the obedience due to him, and which they have probably promised him. They hinder their own progress in the spiritual life, and so hold themselves back from the perfection to which their state of life, or the grace already conferred upon them, obliges them.

Their second privilege is that they may be sure they have not committed mortal sin, unless, with full advertence, they can reverently swear that they have done so. The reason of this is founded on the impossibility of the will's changing unconsciously in one moment from excessive fear to relaxation of morals.

The third privilege of scrupulous persons is that they are not bound to examine matters so exactly as others. The reason for this is that they are spiritual invalids, and the life of an invalid is a life of dispensation, by no less an authority than that of God Himself. The probability is they will never have robust health after this, and therefore the slow strength of convalescence should be assisted. A minute or reiterated examination of conscience or of motives, on the part of a scrupulous man, would be equivalent to the tying and untying of the bandages of a wound, where stillness of the limb and compression of the hurt were just the two things which the surgeon commanded. Neither, as before, are they to be allowed in such fretful examinations without grave cause and the permission of their director. For this privilege, like the rest, must be an obligation in the use.

We certainly care more for our bodies than for our souls. Yet it is only reasonable that what we readily submit to in the case of the one, we should at all events undergo with a good grace in the case of the other. We must prepare our mind to let our spiritual physician treat us when we are sick of scruples. Wonderfully difficult as we think our questions of moral science to be, he will show us no sign of uncertainty or hesitation, and we must doubt whether he has weighed it well or heard us rightly. He will give us no reasons for what he advises, and we must be very open with him, though this will cost us not a little. At the same time, we must have a real abhorrence of exaggerating in confession. This is a common fault of scrupulous persons. They think they make sure of an adequate explanation by an exaggerated one, which is not only an error, but an error on the worst side of the two. Much less mischief would come of an undue extenuation.

He will be very gentle to us while we are docile, but short and abrupt when we are pertinacious. He will not let us repeat things confession after confession, though we are yearning to do so. He will make us learn contempt of our own scruples from his contempt of them. This is as bad as grammar seems to a fourth-grade boy. He will forbid us to confess scruples, and he will accustom us to go to Communion without absolution, which, with our morbid sensitiveness, is worse than great physical pain. He will stint our allowance of time for the examination of our conscience, and we shall consequently go to it at first with such a nervous precipitation, that before we have finished our act of the presence of God, the time will have run out. He will also force upon us a compulsory promptitude in deciding whether to act or not in any particular case, unless the thing looks like a sin at the very first sight of it.

Persons recently converted have scruples about their general confession, either as to its fullness or its sorrow. A spiritual physician will allow them only to reflect generally on their past sins, and very often will prohibit even that. He will never allow them, in a state of scruple, to dwell on particular sins, least of all on circumstances of sins. This is because sadness is a snare which the devil ordinarily sets at this stage of the spiritual life. When their scruples have passed away, he may possibly allow them to make a quiet general confession, and after that, never let them mention anything else belonging to the past, unless they are either wholly without scruple, or able to swear that they have remembered some sin, which they knew to be both mortal and unconfessed. For the sin has been already indirectly remitted.

Scruples fill his veins with the secret poison of self-opinionatedess, just when he has everything to learn and everything to unlearn, and obedience is his sole appointed means of thus changing his whole inner man. Still, it is our comfort to know that the Holy Spirit has reparatory ways and means which evade the definitions of our poor spiritual science, but whose marvelous healing operations we are continually witnessing.

Lastly, there are such things as reasonable scruples. Theology leaves no doubt upon the matter; and nothing of what I have said will apply to them. A prudent fear makes a scruple reasonable, just as a vain fear makes it unreasonable. "You have commanded Your commandments to be kept most diligently", says the Psalmist. A man is not rightly called scrupulous who fears and loves God to a nicety, as the saying is—that is, who strives to avoid every venial sin and every least imperfection. The filial feelings of such men and the tranquility of their solicitude for perfection show that they are not scrupulous in the evil sense. There is such a thing as a wide conscience, and it is wide from the want of reasonable scruples. I only say this to prevent being misunderstood. It will always be better to use the word scruple in a bad sense, and to call reasonable scruples by their much truer and more honorable name of conscientiousness.

Let not the imperfect fear, says St. Augustine, only let them advance. Yet, because I do not let them fear, let them not on that account love imperfection, or remain in it when they have found themselves there. Only let them advance as far as it lies in them, and all is well.

God be praised! We have done, done little certainly, but all we can, for our scrupulous patients. Now let us leave this closed ward, and go out and breathe.

CHAPTER 8

HOW TO RIGHTLY VIEW OUR FAULTS

The sweetest of all the sweet doctrines which St. Francis de Sales was inspired to teach us was that which regarded the right view of our own faults. The consideration of it falls very naturally into this place. On the one hand, we have got clear views of temptations and of scruples, and on the other, a perception of the necessity of an abiding sorrow for sin. That sorrow, as we now understand it, can be no source of scruples, but a right view of our own faults must fall within it and be a part of it. Unfortunately, our faults form a great portion of what we are, and it is plain that their management can be no slight affair in the spiritual life. Rather, our management of them depends very much upon the view we take of them.

Indeed, much of life depends upon taking the right view of things. Time is saved. Mistakes are prevented.

Sometimes we chance upon a short road to Heaven, although short roads are not always the easiest. Strictly speaking, none are short and none are easy, but they may be comparatively so among themselves, and all are full of pleasantness and peace. What do we most abound in? Faults. Perhaps a right view of them may be a short road to Heaven. It will, at any rate, help us to make a road of what looks like a series of barriers.

If a good person were asked to give an account of himself, it would probably be somewhat after the following fashion:

I am constantly doing things which are wrong in themselves. It is not that I do them on purpose, or with forethought. I hope I do not commit any venial sin deliberately. It is the great object of my life, next to loving God, to avoid that.

Yet neither on the other hand can I say that my falls are altogether surprises. They seem so at the time, but not when I come to look back upon them. The sense of guilt grows upon me in the retrospect, rather than reproaches me at the moment. And, worst of all, I see no visible improvement in myself. Again, when I do things which are outwardly right, or, which are even generous, and involve some amount of sacrifice, I continually detect some lowly motive in them. I cannot shake off human respect. Self-love seems inseparable even from my very thoughts, my very sacrifices. It is not as if this happened now and then, but it is going on all day. It runs parallel with the stream of life. I believe I have never done a good work in my life. A spoiled good work is my highest point.

But in prayer I am quite a different person. I seem to have entered another world. I am at my ease and at large. I feel as if I have the aspirations of the saints. Desires of suffering, a desire to suffer calumny, take on tremendous penances, ardent resolutions, or to do heroic deeds, all rush upon me at once, and express precisely what I am feeling most strongly in my interior life. Bold words fill my prayers, though at other times I should have shrunk with reverence. I plead the right of saints, and urge their petitions, and demean myself as if I were one. And all this before God! I do not mean to be insincere. I feel, or I fancy I feel, what I am saying. Yet when I return to my daily practice, I feel as if my prayer had been nothing but hypocrisy from beginning to end. I wish I could think that it were otherwise. There is no sort of proportion between my prayer and my practice. The first is always running ahead of the last, and so absurdly far ahead!

When I come to put generosity in suffering into practice, I fail daily. Then, in with mortifications, they are simply to me what punishments are to a child. It would be as surprising to others as it is humiliating to myself, if I were to mention what little things I do for God, and what a laborious effort it takes to do them, and what immense pain it is. How can I complain, and tremble, and put it off, and hunt for a justifiable dispensation, and sink back into comfortable spirituality, as soon as the momentary effort is over? The revelations I could make of my own pusillanimity, would be almost incredible. But I was grand at prayer in the morning, grand as a martyr at the block in front of one of my own castles in the air.

The upshot of the whole is, that I seem to myself to be getting worse and going back. My sensible fervors have gone, and I do not see that they have left formed habits behind them. I wish I could name any one imperfection that I could say had been effectually weeded out, or any one venial sin, whose crowded ranks had been thinned, or that I could show anything beyond a scratch here and there on my chief passion. All that I can see is that I make as much effort as I used to do, perhaps more, but apparently with less effect.

Now is a person who gives such an account of himself in a good position? On the whole, yes. I found my judgment on two things: 1) The evident desire for perfection with which he began; 2) the fact of continued effort with which he ended. Starting then with these two things, he may reasonably take a consoling view of the rest.

But let us speak of ourselves. Our faults are very numerous and very great: true. But is there anything to surprise us in them? From our own knowledge of ourselves and from what we knew of the measure of our grace, are they not what might have been expected? At times we have thought of our future humbly and prudently, was it very different from what has actually taken place? The fact is that there is nothing astonishing either in the kind or in the degree of our faults. If nothing astonishing, then nothing discouraging. But this is not going far enough. There is something astonishing, and the astonishing thing is that our faults have not been greater. When we weigh ourselves against our temptations, our estimate of things is very different. How unlike ourselves we have happily been in many things! This can be nothing less than the work of grace. Instead of being petulant because we have been so bad, the wonder is that we have been so good, and the fear is lest we should be elated in seeing it.

Common sense also has a word or two to say on the matter. The faults have been committed. They have done their harm, and gone to God. No good is done in being cast down. There is much good in not being so. There is no good in being cast down, because we cannot take back our falls. We may fidget about the circumstances, and worry themselves by thinking how easily the evil might have been avoided. But the fault itself lost us some of our peace—why should we now lose more in self-vexation? Discouragement does not make up any part of penance. It atones for nothing, satisfies for nothing, and merits nothing. It does not make us more careful next time. On the contrary, by dejecting us it makes us at once more open to temptation and less masculine in resisting it. We rather find that there is much good in not being cast down. We shall be less teased with the imperfection in ourselves, and more occupied with the infidelity to God. To fall and not be out of spirits with it is not only to keep the courage we had, but to gain more. It is the humblest course, and on that account the most acceptable to God. It is the most reasonable, and therefore has the greater blessing.

Sometimes a saint gives us a new thought, which we cannot find in any of the spiritual writers before him. It is his contribution to the tradition. When he has said it, it sounds so commonplace that we wonder we never thought of it for ourselves, like the sayings of all great minds. Such a thought is that of St. Francis de Sales, the man of many new thoughts, when he taught us that if in the spiritual life we often fall without perceiving it, so it must be true that we as often get up again without perceiving it. It sounds cliché, but if a man who has the unhappy habit of disquieting himself about his faults would once in a while take it for the subject of his hour's meditation, he would draw from it the very marrow of spiritual wisdom.

We may imagine that we take a sufficiently low view of ourselves, and estimate our achievements, as humility would approve. But any uneasiness about our faults which is more than passing, or a temptation, is a proof to us that we have secretly been putting a far higher price upon ourselves than we should have. And this turning state's evidence against us is the only good such uneasiness ever does, and that is as it were in spite of itself. But does not God occasionally show us fearful things in the depths of our own souls? Sometimes a family with the sunshine of domestic peace and virtue all around it has rented an ancient house for years, when lo! the necessity of some repairs leads to the discovery of secret dungeons and horrible places underground, with traces of misery suffered there, and of guilt perpetrated. It is the same in our own souls. The access of some unusual temptation, the accidental waking up of some long dormant passion, or a flash of supernatural light from God, illuminates for a moment unexplored cavities and unexpected materials for evil.

It may be that the reading or hearing of great crimes may have brought it home to us. But by whatever means we make the discovery, there can be no doubt that we carry about with us immense capabilities of uncommitted sin. Nothing but the merciful turns of a Providence, and the constraining empire of grace, prevent these from being realized in acts. How we crouch under God's mantle, and hold to His feet, when we first get sight of these things! What an amazing, what a blessed disproportion between the evil we do and the evil we are capable of doing, and seem sometimes on the very verge of doing! If my soul has grown weeds, when it was full of seeds of nightshade, how happy ought I to be! And that the weeds have not wholly strangled the wheat, what a wonder it is, an operation of grace, the work of the Sacraments! If a non-Christian emperor thanked God daily for the temptations which He did not allow to approach him, how ought not we to thank Him for the sins we have not committed!

Then, again, do we not experience times in which it seems that grace stirs up the very dregs of our nature, and throws them into a state of fiery effervescence, by some combination of supernatural chemistry? What devils, what beasts we appear to ourselves! For a moment we feel as if we were polluted by the sins which we might have committed, and though a dream, it is all so lifelike that the horrid impression haunts us for days! We are as heavy as if we had very blood upon our souls. At these moments, and without one ounce of vanity or the least fear of complacency, the grateful thought of what we are, the thought which, although it vexes and disheartens us, becomes a pillow of rest to which we turn to forget in the sense of God's mercies the thought of what we might have been, and yet may be. Strange that our little faults should ever be the chosen place of our repose!

Here is another consoling vision. Compare the trifling mixture which we are of God's grace and the human spirit, with what we should be if, without any touch, or taste, or odor of the devil, God left your human spirit simply to itself. The great French spiritual writer, Fr. Olier could not realize this, but God made him see it by removing His assistance from him. He showed him what we should be if He were merely to leave us to ourselves.

"This subtraction takes place," says Fr. Olier, "with regard to sensible grace; for the Divine Goodness does not cease even then to aid us with insensible graces, of a still more efficacious kind. The default of His sensible graces causes strange effects and often prodigious humiliations in the soul. Under the influence of those succors the will and the heart are drawn to God with delight, and something may be observed even in our exterior, the way in which we carry ourselves and the works we do, of an unparalleled sweetness, modesty and equability. When God withdraws these sensible gifts, He leaves the soul in its nakedness, and as great lights came from them before, there is nothing left in the soul now but trouble and confusion. Touched with compassion for my state, God mercifully took these gifts away from me, to show me what I really was, and thus tenderly disabuse me of my error. It is really an effect of huge mercy thus to leave us to ourselves, else we should go on esteeming self, and appropriating to ourselves what belongs to God only, until perhaps we might fall into a blindness like that of Lucifer.

"In this way, God visibly shows to the soul and depths of its own abjection, and so convinces it of its misery. For this sensible grace, which reined in the corrupt man and held him in check, having now retired, everything is changed both in the interior and exterior. The Holy Spirit then leaves him to feel the amount of his natural unruliness and the corruption of his desires. The bridle is thrown upon the neck of the passions. We feel nothing but anger on the slightest occasions, envy, aversions, sentiments of self-love, until our pride breaks out externally in the fierce and haughty expression of our countenance. Yet very often the soul does not at all contribute to this by any thought or voluntary emotion. It is the natural effect of a rising inundation of pride, now that He is gone who could repress it, and bid it hide itself."

A thousand faults that were not mortal sins would be far better than this nature, emancipated from the devil, yet without grace, and enjoying its own wretched prerogatives! See what we are at bottom. Why we are saints compared to our real untempted selves, selves uncompounded with grace and God's compassion!

Although I do not say we ought to be thoroughly contented, we should be fairly happy, if as time goes by we do not add to the kinds of venial sin of which we have to accuse ourselves, nor increase the numbers of those which assault us, nor fall into those with more advertence than before, nor give way more begrudgingly to the surprises of temptation, and still continue to entertain even in our worst times an habitual preference for God. These are five sources of moderate cheerfulness which, while they bring cheer, will not inebriate.

But is it safe and wise to give ourselves up to these considerations? Do we run no risk in thus taking our faults with tranquility? There is a propriety and spiritual wisdom in so doing. What is humble is safe, provided it be true humility. Now, to be indifferent to faults, and to make no endeavor to improve, would not be humility, but lukewarmness or irreligion. It is a very different thing to take our faults with tranquility, and all the while be doing our very best to mend, and wishing intensely to be better. Neither is there any danger of laxity in it, because we are looking to God, and laxity implies a downward, not an upward eye. It leads us away from self. Even self-love makes us hate self. All this taking of our faults with tranquility is in reality based upon a supernatural principle, which both implies and augments interior mortification.

Moreover, this tranquility is an absolutely necessary for spiritual growth under ordinary circumstances. There are sometimes brief storms in the interior when we grow, like children during an illness. It is plain that tranquility must be the prevailing atmosphere of an ascetic. We must be quiet in order to pray. Mortification must be tranquil, or else it will be merely vehement nature, growing in fury as it grows in pain. Confidence in God must be tranquil. The very word itself is full of the sound of rest. The receiving of the Sacraments must be tranquil. Noise and hurry would be simple irreverence. Our love of others must be tranquil, else it will degenerate into earthly tenderness. In a word, there is hardly a function of the spiritual life which does not require tranquility for its exercise and fulfillment. Yet faults are universal, daily, in all subject matters, thought, word, deed, look, and omission. They cover the whole surface of life incessantly, so that if we do not take them with tranquility, we shall never be tranquil at all. This is so absurd a result that it is as good as a demonstration that we must take our faults with tranquility.

The desire of perfection is, as we have already seen, a gift from God, and a great gift, seeing that a generous and earnest pursuit of virtue is necessary to perfection. Yet we must not be inordinately attached either to the desire or the pursuit. If it is God's will to hold us back, we must be content to be held back. The goodness of a thing is no justification of an unruly eagerness in acquiring it. The eagerness of the pursuit will more than counterbalance the blessing of the acquisition. Our falls are permitted. Our share in them must be wiped away by cheerful, hopeful sorrow. The rest God will look to, and we must be at peace.

There is also this other disadvantage in the opposite line of conduct. Discouragement necessarily brings with it a greediness for consolation. The more we are disturbed, the more we run to what will give solace and soothe us. This is bringing back self again into everything, besides disarming us before the genuine struggle, and giving us a distaste for mortification. Consolations from creatures never really help, but very often hinder; and an appetite for them is a bad augury of progress.

But in the spiritual life there is never a permission without a caution, never a relaxation without a saving clause against laxity. So, in this case we must be careful to distinguish hopefulness from self-conceit. To be quiet under our faults is not to be free and easy with them— cheerfulness is a very different thing from vanity. But how to discern between the two? Hope implies a certain amount of doubt, and that again implies fear. When we hope in time to advance beyond the circle of particular faults, we have some, but a subordinate fear that possibly we may not succeed.

That fear is plainly self-distrust, and it is subordinate, else it would be discouragement. Conceit has no fear, because it has no doubt, and no hope, because it does not contemplate its success as being in any way uncertain. Thus, self-distrust is one test by which we can distinguish hopefulness from conceit. A confidence in God more than equaling our distrust of self is another sign. Conceit trusts in itself, and in its reckonings calculates as a right what humility sees to be a grace.

A third test is to be found in the gradual growth of the supernatural in our feelings, motives and desires. If we look more to God, if we lean more upon Sacraments, if we prefer the divine will to our own spiritual advancement, then we may be sure that our tranquility with our faults is hopefulness, and not conceit.

The whole question comes to this. There are two views of growth in grace, the self-help view and the will of God view. In these views—for what is more operative than a view—is the root of all the error and of all the wisdom of the matter. If a man puts self-help before him as the end of life, almost every step that he takes will be wrong. If he works away at himself, as a sculptor finishes off a statue, he will get more out of proportion, and the longer he chisels, he will bring out more black marks and gray blotches. Not a motive will be right, not an aim true. If he takes up his particular examination and his rule of life, and his periodical penances, as merely medicinal appliances, if he shuts himself up in a reformatory school of his own, if he models his whole spiritual life upon the complacent theory of self-help, his asceticism will be nothing better than a systematizing and a glorifying of self-will. Under such auspices he can never be a spiritual man, and he will hardly be a moral man. Yet how common is this miserable view, even among men living right in the heart of a system so intensely supernatural as that of the Catholic Church!

The will of God view, on the contrary, refers everything but diligence and correspondence to Him. A man follows God's lead, and does not strike out a road for himself. He models himself in his measure and degree on the imitation of Jesus. He seeks to please God, and acts out of love. His inconsistencies neither astonish nor tease him. An imperfection annoys him, not because it mars the symmetry of his character, but because it grieves the Holy Spirit. Sacraments, and scapulars, and beads and medals, relics and rites, all find their places in his system. Both the natural and the supernatural form one whole. God is always pleased when a man seeks humbly, and in appointed ways, to please Him. Hence this man is tranquil, cheerful and hopeful with his faults. The cheerfulness of endless success is in his heart. God is his Father. Whereas the self-help man either does not succeed in helping himself, or he does so too slowly, or he loses on one side what he gains on the other, or people will persist in being scandalized at his edifying deportment, for with such men edification is the crown of virtue, and if they do not edify, they have foiled. As a result, he is spasmodic, sulky and desponding about his faults. The bitterness of endless piecemeal failure is in his heart.

After death we shall have many revelations. I suspect the hiddenness of our spiritual growth here on earth will give rise to some. How surprised many humble spirits will be at the extraordinary beauty of their souls, when death has disengaged them! So much more is always going on than we in the least suspect!